The
Don't Get Me Started!
Toolkit

Strategies

for a

Culturally-Challenged World

Patricia Kutza and Connie Payne

ORDERING INFORMATION

QUANTITY SALES. Special discounts are available on quantity purchases by corporations, associations, and others. Contact dgmskp@gmail.com

INDIVIDUAL SALES: This publication can be purchased at Amazon.com or ordered by contacting the authors at dgmskp@gmail.com

ORDERS FOR COLLEGE TEXTBOOK/COURSE ADOPTION USE: Please contact the authors at dgmskp@gmail.com

ISBN-13: 978-0692705711
ISBN-10: 0692705716

The Don't Get Me Started! Toolkit   Strategies for a Culturally-Challenged World

Kutza, Patricia and Payne, Connie

First Edition

Cover design: Patricia Kutza and Connie Payne. Cover illustration: Patricia Kutza and Connie Payne All interior illustrations: Patricia Kutza and Connie Payne

DEDICATION

To our sisters of inspiration, spirit and guidance
-- Mary Collet and Paulette Newborn --

CONTENTS

ACKNOWLEDGMENTS

We would like to thank Herman Alston and Alvin Payne for their patience during the long hours we spent creating this book. We would also like to thank Elisa Kutza and Mary Collet for their constructive *Don't Get Me Started!* critiques. And Natalya for napping at just the right time.

INTRODUCTION

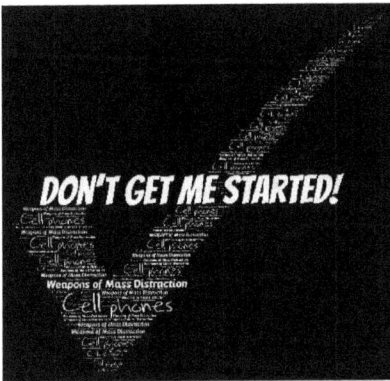

Recently Connie and I were walking together on a very busy street and a man approached us. He wasn't looking directly at either of us and was talking loudly while his arms flailed at his sides. As he got closer to us, we could tell from his comments that he was conversing with someone over his mobile phone (while using a hands-free connection). We passed each other while he continued to gesture broadly and we could still hear him conversing when we were then about a ½ block away from him.

Connie turned to me and said: "Don't Get Me Started!" It's become our shared mantra –the phrase that we recite to each other every time we experience behavior that goes beyond any expectation or norm that we consider how a reasonable and socially intelligent person would act in a similar situation. It wasn't very long ago that, upon seeing and hearing that man approaching us, we would quickly walk to the other side of the street, assuming that he was mentally ill or on drugs. But that was before wireless cell phone technology entered our lives. Now we immediately assume that persons talking out loud to no visible persons are talking on their mobile devices.

It's really a paradigm-shift and points to something far deeper and more important happening in our globally-connected society. The convergence of rapidly changing technologies, evolving social mores and shifting cultural demographics triggered by immigration patterns is creating unprecedented challenges to the conventional norms that have traditionally regulated our expectations about acceptable social behavior.

The Death of Mother Wit?

At times it seems that these challenges have so eclipsed contemporary society that the core trait that used to run through social behavior, the practice of common sense, has evaporated into the ether. Road rage and reckless Twitter-based shaming rants are just a few of the indicators that a cultural cluelessness has taken over in the vacuum left by the retreat of common sense.

In times of great social upheaval during the last four centuries, etiquette books have provided the guidance that folks sought to get their cultural bearings and be assured safe passage among and between cultures. The present cultural cluelessness epidemic points to the fact that these books no longer adequately address societal needs for cultural advice. Today cultural transformations, fueled by technological advances, evolving social mores, shifting immigration patterns and generational and racial differences, are vastly changing our expectations about what we consider 'proper' behavior, making it less likely that folks can successfully rely on traditional etiquette books, that offer broad brush-stroked advice, to ground themselves socially.

We believe that these transformations, while offering great opportunities for social change, also require more of the citizens of this world. They require people to adopt new habits of thinking , listening and responding that will help them better navigate a world where the conventional rules governing the boundaries of private and public behavior are often ambiguous.

In *Don't Get Me Started!* we offer a toolkit of skills for skillfully assessing and responding to the many challenging situations you may encounter in this rapidly changing world. So whether you are playing games online, using a 'gender-free' restroom, sharing a picture on Facebook, conversing with friends in a café, applying in person for a new job or hosting an intergenerational event – you will be able to determine how the rules have changed and act in a manner that assures more successful outcomes.

Exercising the skills of our toolkit daily, and possibly multiple times each day, may seem difficult, especially when you are required to respond in a matter of seconds. But in one form or another, most of us already use these skills. Our goal in writing this book is to bring conscious awareness to the process, and to suggest tips on how you can keep refining the process.

What is this Thing called Culture?

Culture is one of those words that means different things to different people. To some it conjures images of specific nationalities, or geographic-specific customs. Others may immediately think about generational differences.

For readers of *The Don't Get Me Started! Toolkit, Strategies for a Culturally Challenged World,* we think it is critical for you to know just what we mean by this word.

For purposes of this book, we define the word 'culture' quite broadly. It includes:

- The shared understandings people use within a society to align their actions.
- The ways a group of people solve problems and reconcile dilemmas.
- The patterns of thinking and feeling that people use when facing various situations and actions.

In fact, visualize 'culture' as a very large circle. Its fabric is composed of shared understandings, problem-solving strategies and patterns of thinking/feeling/reacting. Now visualize smaller circles within this circle—some of them are concentrically nested within each other...some of them overlap The circles within the main circle (culture) represent different culture groupings:

- Work environments (eg. Company cultures)

- Generations (such as baby boomers, millennials, etc)
- Nationalities /Races
- Public spaces

All people throughout their lives are a part of at least three culture groupings: Their nationality/race, their generation and those of their parents and their experiences in public places. Many of them work outside their homes so they also experience a company culture.

If you look closely at every one of these cultural groupings, you will find specific understandings, problem-solving strategies and patterns of thinking and feeling that inform these communities. And what holds this fabric together is a body of rules that keeps these groupings cohesive.

This body of rules is most frequently called **etiquette.** Some readers, at this point, may balk at the word, feeling that etiquette is for 'other' people and an 'other' time when rules of decorum held sway. What can etiquette possibly offer a world whose attitudes and mores are changing at a breathless pace?

We offer the theory that if you aspire to thrive as a productive and valued member of your community, you cannot afford to ignore knowing how the skillful application of etiquette can help you achieve these goals within all these cultural groupings.

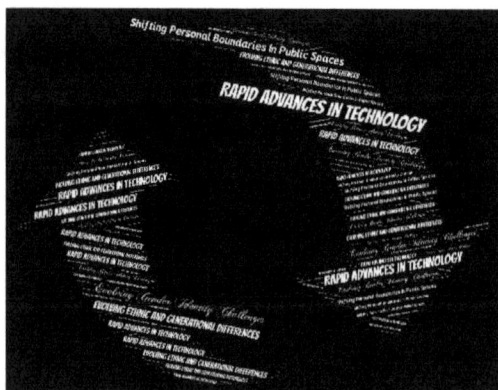

We Are Not Saying That It Will Be Easy

We will be the first ones to testify that learning how to skillfully navigate in a world where many people seem to reject the conventional rules of etiquette is *not* easy! In fact the challenge facing all of us --- to be able to seamlessly understand and adapt to multiple rules of etiquette – is quite difficult. This is because the rules of etiquette are not always easily discernible and sometimes clash when culture groupings converge.

Additionally there are many forces in our world that continue to make this task so tricky. They include:

- ✓ **Rapid advances in technology** that are constantly disrupting entrenched rules of etiquette. . Technological advances have far outstripped many users' abilities to comprehend the power –both beneficial and destructive – that these new ways of connecting affect their lives.

- ✓ **Evolving generational and ethnic differences.** The generational fault lines are shifting. Forces contributing to this shifting are rooted in technological advances, economics and values (priorities) hierarchies. For instance, the trend that workers need to 'brand' themselves is a relatively recent phenomenon, a given for millennials and generation Y folks who now must compete with a global work force, largely made accessible by the rapid adoption of the World Wide Web.

  Their embrace of social media as one of their primary 'branding' tools offers benefits but is also fraught with challenges. Additionally people are also far more likely to live and work in communities that are more culturally diverse than when and where they were born or grew up. This diversity offers many opportunities for growth. But it also presents challenges when conflicting attitudes and beliefs co-exist.

- ✓ **Evolving attitudes about gender identity.** Increased acceptance of same sex marriage is also paving the way for a broader acceptance of transgender rights that often challenges deeply-seated conceptions about gender definitions and expressions of gender identity.

✓ **Shifting personal boundaries in public spaces**. The boundaries that traditionally define acceptable public and private behaviors are shifting. For instance, prior to the advent of mobile phones, a person talking to himself in public would have been considered on the fast path to the looney bin. According to Pew Research Center over 75% of adults now feel that it is perfectly acceptable to converse on their phones in public spaces. The problem is that many people act totally clueless –talking loudly and broadcasting intimate private details about their lives --when using their mobile devices in public places.

The upshot of all these cultural challenges is the fact that a new model for etiquette –that goes beyond traditional etiquette –is needed to keep our public-behavior-wheels turning smoothly. Without it, daily life will continue to be a mine-field where people stumble culturally-- creating the impression that they are 'culturally clueless'.

Being 'culturally-clueless' may not land you in jail…but it could very well make you less competitive in the job marketplace, less admired among your peers and less respected within your family.

The Antidote to Being 'Culturally Clueless': Being 'Culturally Tuned In'

The great thing about being 'culturally-tuned-in' is that you don't have to remember any rules per se, adhere to a strict code of conduct or be eminently knowledgeable about the multitude of customs extant in our world.

From our perspective, no one really has the inside track on the best or smartest way to behave in all circumstances. Circumstances are fluid and there may be no absolute *right* way to behave all the time.

However we have observed over time that there are certain abilities that 'culturally-tuned-in' people share. They demonstrate high degrees of:

- **Emotional intelligence** (ability to empathize with others)
- **Critical thinking** (ability to test and reassess current beliefs and assumptions)
- **Flexibility** (ability to adapt to situations outside of comfort zone)
- **Creativity** (ability to find new ways to interact)

These abilities help them navigate successfully through the interlocking rules of etiquette that inform our various culture groupings.

We believe that all of these abilities can be learned and with continual practice become those skills that 'culturally-tuned-in' people rely on when they encounter situations in life that test their patience, intelligence and willingness to change. They are the foundation of our *Don't Get Me Started! Toolkit.*

We will be talking about these skills in depth a little later in this book. In the next chapter we talk about the many challenges that make learning how to practice these abilities so important.

The Don't Get Me Started! Toolkit!

Chapter 1

Challenges to Being 'Culturally-Tuned-In'

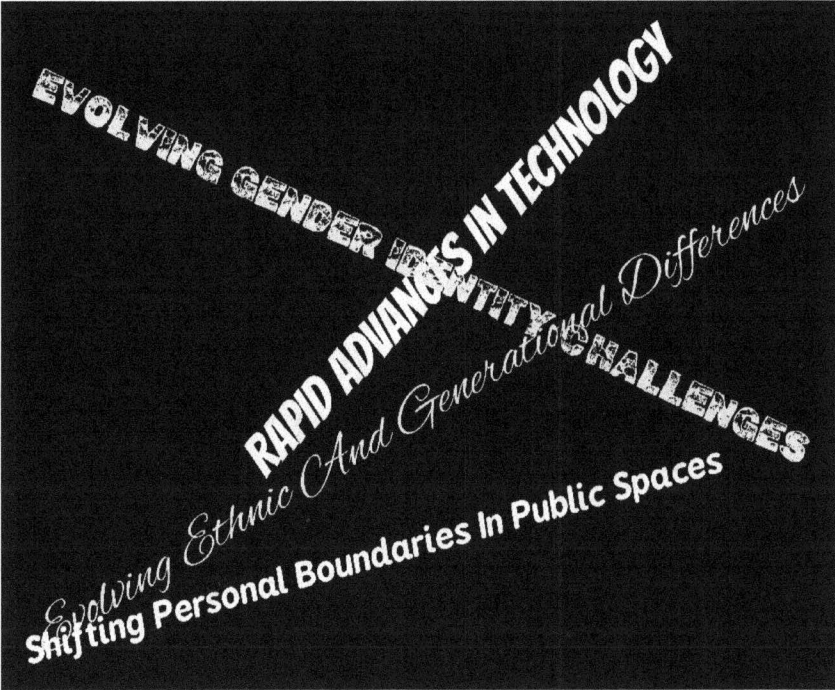

EVOLVING GENDER IDENTITY CHALLENGES

RAPID ADVANCES IN TECHNOLOGY

Evolving Ethnic And Generational Differences

Shifting Personal Boundaries In Public Spaces

Rapid Advances in Technology

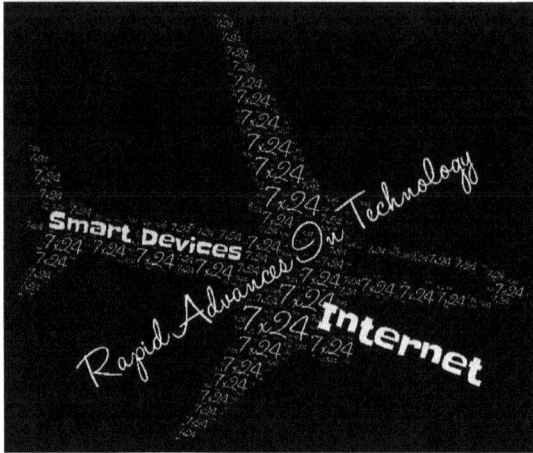

Compared to the present, it was a very different world in the 1920s that welcomed the first etiquette missives written by the woman whose name would become synonymous with manners – Emily Post. Her syndicated columns became a popular feature of newspapers – Readers couldn't wait to read her next installment. And they probably also couldn't wait to grab a pen and paper and write letters to their family and friends – asking for their opinions about Ms. Post's latest admonitions or instructions.

Rapid advances in technology have exponentially increased the ways we now communicate. Some predict that newspapers, at least those made from pulp, are in terminal decline. And very few people can actually remember receiving a handwritten letter within the last six months. Now 'smart' devices – in conjunction with the 'always on' capabilities of the Internet, - via chat, video conferencing, email and messaging (texting) -- give folks myriad ways to connect.

Connecting 24/7

And connect they do….24/7….. around the clock and around the world. Few would argue that no other technological invention has made such a profound paradigm shift as the Internet. It is a force that has become the great leveler – making the online playing field accessible to both the largest of corporations and the most obscure of individuals—all being able to voice their opinions and interests.

But with all the Internet's power that expands our horizons comes this inconvenient truth: Technological advances have far outstripped many users' abilities to comprehend the impact - both beneficial and destructive – that these new opportunities to connect with others represent in their lives.

Offering Blessings and Curses

Nowhere is this truth more evident than in the often unfettered and often clueless ways that users interact with social media. They frequently *overshare* details about themselves and others, showing an inability to comprehend the multiplier effect of online communication. One of the most powerful examples of this effect can be seen in the destructive power unleashed by Twitter users when they 'pile-on' negative comments.

Bullying – a phenomenon as old as life itself – takes on a new dimension on the Net. The emotional aspect of Internet content is amplified, giving its perpetrators heightened powers.

Coupled with the cult and worship of celebrity (the addiction to grabbing 15 minutes of online fame) the virtual Internet world offers a parallel universe that has a life of its own.

The challenge to staying 'culturally tuned in' is to be able to leverage the wonderful opportunities to connect that the Internet offers without buying into the notion that the Net is a wild frontier where no rules of etiquette apply. They still do…and the folks who break them get smacked while the whole world is watching.

Evolving Generational and Ethnic Differences

The generational fault-lines are shifting. Forces contributing to this shifting are rooted in technological advances, changing economics and evolving value systems. Historically a new generation emerges every twenty years. Longer life

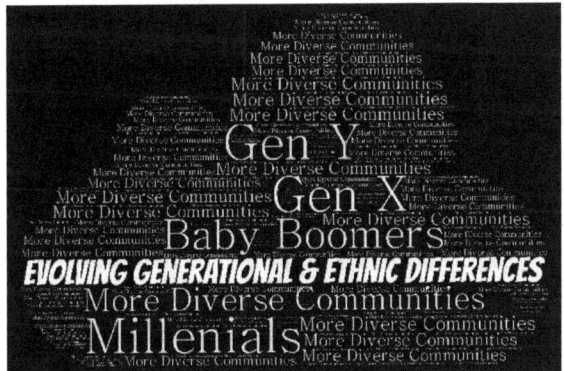

expectancy is contributing to the presence of more generations inhabiting the world at one time.

Currently these generations include:

Traditionalist – born before 1946

Baby Boomers – 1946 – 1964

Generation X – 1965 – 1976

Generation Y / Millennials – 1977 and beyond

Each generation tends to have certain characteristics in common. Increasingly these characteristics are shaped by seismic shifts caused by changing world views and access to technology.

The book *Flex*[1] describes some of these differences. Baby Boomers, for example, traditionally respect authority, even if they do not respect the person the authority is tied to. Generation X, eager to voice their opinion, are still prone to follow the directives of the person in authority. Generation Y, or Millennials, tend to be receptive to hearing the reasons behind a decision or judgement. If the motivation seems authentic, they will generally follow through. However, if the policy is the equivalent of "because I say so," then they tend to push back rather than conform, feeling that this policy is inherently disrespectful to them.

Online Differentiator

Perhaps more than any other factor, familiarity and dexterity with technology defines the differences between the current generations. Millennials, more than any other generation, rely on technology as their preferred means of communication, i.e. texting, e-mails, Twitter, chats etc. In many cases, online modes of communicating replace face-to-face encounters. This reliance on online communication can put millennials at a distinct disadvantage when applying for jobs where being able to effectively communicate face-to-face is a valued skill. Having so many online-based ways to communicate also can

---

[1] Jane Hyun, and Audrey S. Lee, <u>Flex</u>: <u>The New Playbook for Managing Across Differences</u>. (New York: HarperBusiness, 2014)

create confusion and frustration between the generations when one mode such as Facebook is the preferred medium. Users may feel forced to adopt its use, whether they like it or not, in order to 'stay in the loop.'

Branding from Cradle to Grave

Another relatively new phenomenon, driven largely by technology, is the concept of branding. Scrapbooks, photographs and travel slide shows have been traditional ways for earlier generations to 'curate' their lives. The youngest of generations now, with their selfies and videos, begin their branding campaigns much earlier. Social media, one of their primary branding tools, provides a double-edged sword. It offers an array of benefits, but is also fraught with challenges. Before hiring applicants, employers often vet them online to see how effectively (or not) these potential employees 'brand' their identities on the Internet.

Whether they are age four, 40 or 84, Web users are still sorting out the disconnects between what is considered 'acceptable' behavior on and offline. The book *So You Have Been Publicly Shamed*[2] equates the Net to the Wild West, the place where netizens can act out in ways for which they would be penalized offline. Are these 'new freedoms' really shackles in disguise?

As the World Wide Web continues to evolve, along with political, economic and social change, there are bound to be many more 'shakeups' as these generational fault lines shift!

More Diverse Communities

Compared to almost a half century ago, people are far more likely to live in communities that are more culturally diverse than when and where they were born or grew up.

According to USA Today's article, "Second Immigration Wave Lifts Diversity to Record High," the U.S. is experiencing its' 'second great wave' of immigration[3]. The first great wave, stretched from the

---

[2] Jon Ronson, <u>So You Have Been Publicly Shamed,</u> (New York: Riverhead Books, 2016)

1880's to the 1920's. It coincided with the opening of Ellis Island, and the social and political transformation of the nation. The second great wave began roughly around 1970.

USA Today's census data-based Diversity Index rates every U.S. county on a scale of 0-100. Nationwide, the Diversity Index hit 55 in 2014, up sharply from 20 in 1960, and 40 in 1990. It is predicted to reach or exceed 70 by 2060. The U.S. Department of Education reports that public schools began the 2014-2015 school year with an unprecedented profile: Ethnic minorities exceeded white students in public school enrollment across the nation.

Immigration is projected to be the key driver of national population growth in the coming half century, per a Pew Research Center report.[4] Higher birth rates are tied to the expectation that immigrants from other countries will continue their tendency to bear more children than native born residents.

As people from varying cultures and races merge within our society, local governments, the workplace, and other institutions must deal with a host of new issues. Immigrants bring with them traditions, customs and beliefs that may challenge the cultural mores of the communities where they resettle. Culturally-tuned-in people tend to concentrate on similarities among cultures without glossing over the differences.

Evolving Gender Identity Challenges

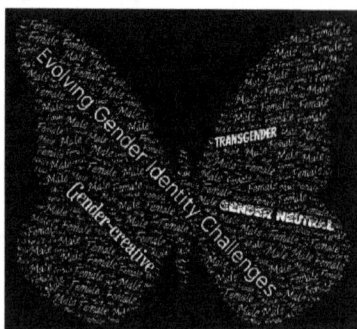

We live in a computer-driven world where the '0s' and '1s' of digital currency inform so much of our society. But way before the language of computers transformed our lives, we were embedded with hard-coded beliefs – that what defines the male

---

[3] Greg Toppo and Paul Overberg, "Second Immigration Wave Lifts Diversity to Record High", 21 October 2014, USA Today.com.

[4] Cohn, D'vera. "Future Immigration with change the face of America by 2065", 05 October 2015. FactTank, PewResearch.org.

and female sexes are immutable definitions.

"In our world, gender is bedrock - the way we ground ourselves with each other. For example, when a woman is expecting a baby - the first question on everybody's lips is 'Is it a boy or a girl?'" says Diane Ehrensaft, a developmental and clinical psychologist who specializes in gender studies and psychotherapy. She describes the current transgender rights movement as a huge cultural shift, creating challenges that often go to the core of deeply-seated conceptions about gender and expressions of gender identity

"We are now asked to comprehend that gender can be many shades[5] and also that it need not be permanent" Ehrensaft explains. "The sensibility that a person can be gender-neutral is like a moving boulder under this bedrock. Think of these cultural changes as a gender mosaic which is in essence like a stream of these moving boulders - some of which clash with each other. - and the challenge is to find a way to feel grounded in this new paradigm."

Nuanced Concepts

People who seek to broaden their understanding of the transgender movement quickly realize that the concepts are nuanced. Many identities fall under the transgender umbrella, says the American Psychological Association.[6] And the associated terms usually but not always describe the differences.

---

[5] In her book *Gender Born, Gender Made*, Dr. Diane Ehrensaft created the term 'gender creative' to describe children whose unique gender expression or sense of identity is not defined by a checkbox on their birth certificate

[6] "Answers to Your Questions about Transgender People, Gender Identity and Gender Expression", American Psychological Association.org.

For example the term *transsexual* refers to people whose gender identity is different from their assigned sex. Transsexuals may alter their bodies through hormones, surgery, and other means to make their bodies in sync as possible with their gender identities. This process is called sex or gender reassignment, and more recently, gender affirmation. Some individuals who transition from one gender to another prefer to be referred to as a man or a woman, rather than as transgender. All these definitions underscore the reality that cookie-cutter approaches will not suffice to illustrate this paradigm shift in gender identity expression.

Words Matter

As the American Psychological Association cautions at their website: "While transgender is generally a good term to use, not everyone whose appearance or behavior is gender-nonconforming will identify as a transgender person. The ways that transgender people are talked about in popular culture, academia and science are constantly changing, particularly as individuals' awareness, knowledge and openness about transgender people and their experiences grow." Words do matter and increasingly it will be true that a sign of a culturally-tuned in person will be one who understands the militancy of the new gender identity mantra that says: "My pronouns are mandatory, not preferred!"

Shifting Private Boundaries in Public Spaces

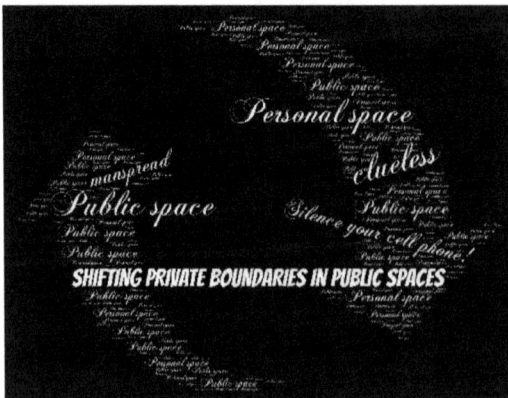

In what are commonly considered 'public' spaces, people are increasingly behaving in ways that in previous times would have been relegated to 'private' spaces. This is a phenomenon partly due to changes in social communication patterns as well as the wide-spread adoption of new technologies.

In the work world of the last half of the twentieth century, cubicles (also known as 'cubes') gave workers their own private space. The current emphasis on effective team collaboration as a major business strategy is reflected in the open architecture design of newer companies or the redesign of legacy firms. Cubes are often replaced by open space where teams of workers can cluster together.

Going Mobile

The proliferation of mobile devices has introduced a new behavior paradigm that challenges further the traditional notion that private behavior needs private space. Before the era of mobile devices, phone booths in public spaces gave phone users the very tangible feeling that they were talking in private – and because these enclosures muffled the sound of their speech - others outside the booth perceived it as such. Now, though it is increasingly harder to find a phone booth in many countries, judging from the often inappropriate volume of mobile phone users' conversations, it would seem that these phone users feel, even without the privacy of phone booths, that they are still in an invisible cocoon that separates and shield them from others.

Invisible Boundaries

This shifting understanding of what is permissible public and private behavior and the often surprising cluelessness of users is also glaringly apparent in their behavior in the virtual public space inhabited by social media. Pre-Internet, many people who might have been very guarded about the details of their private lives are now sharing the most intimate details about themselves. It is as if they regard the World Wide Web as one huge social club where everyone has the best of intentions. It only takes one malicious comment on a forum such as Reddit or Facebook to unleash a fury of vitriol that challenges the validity of such a notion.

Judging from the often 'clueless' behavior in both physical and virtual public spaces, it is apparent to us that people are only in the very nascent stages of sorting out how to respect the invisible yet very real private boundaries that surround them when they are operating in the public spaces of both the physical and virtual worlds. We feel that a new etiquette that keeps our public-behavior-wheels turning smoothly is not yet codified - it's not an expectation that is implicitly understood by many people. Still it is a yardstick that people often unconsciously use when they judge whether a person is culturally-tuned-in.

Chapter 2

Cultural IQ Test

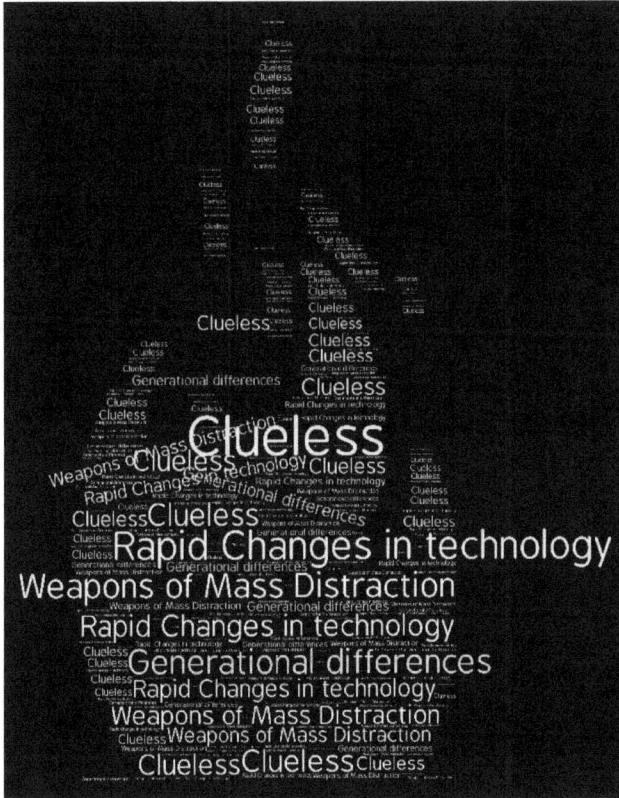

Here's a short quiz that will test your level of being culturally-tuned-in. As you compare your answers with ours, notice how engaging our toolkit of abilities offers new ways to engage positively in a variety of situations.   We hope that participating in this exercise will whet your curiosity to read our book further when we tackle thornier scenarios that often challenge folks, and share with you how exercising our toolkit skills – critical thinking, emotional intelligence, creativity and flexibility - makes the likelihood of behaving in a culturally tuned-in way, much more likely.

TEST QUESTIONS

Question#1

Consider this case of over-sharing

Rhoda's middle school classmate dares her to take a very revealing 'selfie' and post it on Instagram. *What should she do?*

    A. Rhoda should never take revealing 'selfies.'

    B. Rhoda should only share revealing 'selfies' with trusted friends.

    C. Rhoda should never share revealing 'selfies' with anyone

    D. Revealing 'selfies' should be deleted after they are sent to the intended receiver.

Question#2

Encountering personal fundraising in the work place

Jana, a new employee at an accounting firm, is single whereas most of the employees are married and have children. Practically every month, there are multiple solicitations from workers who are promoting their children's school programs; management included. Jana feels this tradition has gone beyond what is reasonable, and also feels it is unprofessional. *What should Jana do?*

    A: To be fair, Jana should try to buy something from each fundraiser.

    B. Jana should buy items from the children in management.

    C. Jana should choose the months that she wants to participate in purchasing items from the fundraisers, and make this known to all in the office.

    D. Jana should not participate in the purchasing of item for fundraising, and she should let her feelings regarding the practice be known to those in the office.

Question #3

Dealing with pungent fragrances in the work place

Sandra works in a small office with two other women. The three women work well together. However, there is one problem. One of the women frequently wears a very pungent fragrance. The scent is so strong, it permeates the entire office. This has made working very uncomfortable for Sandra. *What should Sandra do?*

A.   Keep the windows and doors open .
B.   Politely and privately mention to her co-worker that her fragrance affects her.
C.   Grin and bear it.
D.   Report the issue to her boss.

Question #4

Using social media prudently

Sean, a social media buff, recently experiences a home break-in while on vacation. Sean lives in an upper middle class neighborhood, and this is his second break-in while on vacation. *Which option/s should Sean consider following?:*

A.   Beware of modern technology. Temporarily discontinue technology that allows access to the entrance of his home when he is away for an extended amount of time.

B.   Limit the information he posts on-line regarding his whereabouts, especially when he will be away for an extended amount of time.

C.   A and B

D.   Limit the amount of vacation photos he posts on-line.

Question #5

Follow me following you

Allesse attends a wedding reception, which includes a buffet of a variety of food items. Allesse is standing toward the end of the buffet line. There are approximately 80 people in front of her and approximately 30 additional people behind her. As she approaches the food, she notices a number of buffet trays are almost empty. *Considering there are 30 people behind her, what should Allesse do?*

    A. Take only a small amount from each tray containing the food she desires.
    B. Fill her plate with the items from the trays that are not almost empty.
    C. Refrain from taking items from the trays that were almost empty.
    D. Notify the serving staff that there is not enough food .

Question #6

Facing a weapon of mass distraction

Patti unexpectedly runs into Cary, an acquaintance of hers, who she has not seen in a while. During their brief 'catch-up session,' Cary's cell phone rings. Cary answers her phone, and without excusing herself, proceeds to talk for several minutes, giving no indication to Patti of how much longer she will be talking on her phone. Feeling slighted, Patti turns around and walks away. *What is Cary's breech of etiquette?*

    A. Cary should have said, "Excuse me", before taking the call.
    B. Cary should have let the call go to voice-mail.
    C. Cary should have asked the caller if she could call her back.
    D. A and C

Question #7

Facing the snail

Ron volunteers to organize the next family reunion. His guest list is extensive, spanning three generations of family members. Many of his family members have Facebook accounts. *What is the best way for Ron to disperse his invitations?*

A. Ron should post his reunion invitation on Facebook, and instruct the Facebook members to spread the word to those who do not have Facebook accounts.
B. Ron should make phone calls to invite the guests.
C. Ron should use an e-mail based application to send to his guest, since more of his guests might have e-mail than Facebook.
D. Ron should send invitations by snail mail. He can also post the invitation on Facebook, and send a mass e-mail.

Question #8

The photographer wears many hats

A photographer asks Jamal, a young African-American, to take off his hat for a group photo. He tells Jamal that it is blocking the face of the person behind him. Jamal refuses to remove his hat. *What should the photographer do?*

A. He should not take the picture until Jamal removes his hat.
B. He should ask Jamal to move to another location in the picture.
C. He should ask the person standing behind Jamal to move to a different location.
D. He should simply proceed with the picture and disregard Jamal's hat.

Question #9

A cornucopia of food options

Justin, the group supervisor of an office of approximately 20 employees, is responsible for planning the Christmas Party. He wants to improve upon last year's some-what unpopular choice of assorted sandwiches, fruit, and cookies. However, upon reviewing the dietary needs of his staff, he discovers the planning will be much more difficult than he had anticipated. Justin finds that his staff consists of five different ethnic groups, two vegans, three vegetarians, a diabetic, and one lactose intolerant employee. *How should Justin approach this dilemma?*

    A. Enlist the help of a caterer to develop a menu and prepare the food.

    B. Plan a pot-luck, allowing each employee to sign up for entrees, appetizers, and desserts.

    C. Provide several diverse menus, and allow the staff to vote on their preferred one.

    D. Stick with the menu that was used the year before.

Question #10

Guess which guest

Sarah is invited to high tea by her friend Tina. However, Sarah has also agreed to go to lunch and attend a church function with another friend on the same day. The events are approximately two and a half hours apart. Sarah could attend both events, if she is mindful of the time factor of each. Sarah really wants to attend both. *What would be the best approach to solving this dilemma?*

    A. Sarah could forego lunch and meet her friend at the church after attending Tina's tea. Then perhaps go to dinner after the church event with her church friend.

    B. Sarah could choose between the two events which to attend.

C. In order to avoid a negative response, Sarah and her church friend could forego lunch, and attend Tina's tea, then attend the church event.

D. Sarah could call Tina, and ask if it would be acceptable to bring her church friend with her to the tea, then attend the church event.

Cultural IQ Test Answers

As you compare your answers with ours, notice that the abilities of critical thinking, emotional intelligence, flexibility and creativity that we discuss in our introduction are included in our analysis of these test answers. This entire toolkit of skills will be covered in depth in the next chapter and throughout the rest of this book.

Question#1 - **A case of over-sharing**

Correct Answer: A - Rhoda should never take revealing 'selfies.' (20pts.)

Commentary: Choice A uses critical thinking, emotional intelligence and flexibility – 3 of the 4 abilities in our toolkit:

- ✓ Critical Thinking: A logically-thinking Rhoda considers the potential consequences of her actions. She understands that the negatives far outweigh the positives.
- ✓ Emotional Intelligence: Using her emotional intelligence Rhoda understands that she has options for stroking her self-esteem.
- ✓ Flexibility: Although Rhoda is tempted to accept the dare of taking the revealing 'selfie', she opts, instead, to be flexible. She refrains from exposing herself to vulnerability in exchange for popularity.

Choice C   Rhoda should never share revealing 'selfies' with anyone (15pts)

This would be the next best choice, because Rhoda would have used:

- Critical Thinking: Rhoda does critically consider the pitfalls of sharing revealing 'selfies', but does not extend her thought process far enough. She does not consider the possibility of someone gaining access to her phone and the photos stored in it. Furthermore, Rhoda does not consider the possibility that the person who gains such access might pornographically alter the 'selfie', and send it to others.

- Emotional Intelligence : By refraining from sharing revealing 'selfies,' Rhoda decreases her vulnerability, and does not put herself in the position of relying on the integrity of others.

- Flexibility: Here Rhoda shows some flexibility. She decides to continue taking revealing 'selfies,' but will not share them. However, as previously mentioned, Rhoda has not considered the flaw in this resolution – others gaining access without her knowledge or permission.

Choice B: Rhoda should only share revealing 'selfies' with trusted friends. (10pts)

This choice somewhat addresses:

- Emotional Intelligence: There is some attempt to limit vulnerability, but Rhoda still risks the possibility of experiencing that social behavior called "Friends today, foes tomorrow."

- Flexibility: Rhoda has devised a plan to limit her exposure – only showing revealing 'selfies' to trusted friends. However had she used critical thinking she would have identified the flaws in this approach.

Choice D: Revealing 'selfies' should be deleted after they are sent to the intended receiver. (5pts)

This choice shows some sense of:

- Emotional Intelligence: Again, Rhoda does acknowledge the need to limit her vulnerability. She understands the potential repercussions of the revealing 'selfie' if accessed by an unintended receiver.

- Flexibility: Rhoda devises a plan to limit her vulnerability. However she doesn't use critical thinking which would reveal the flaws of this plan.

- Creativity: Rhoda's plan to delete the 'selfie' - to avoid an unintended receiver accessing it - is an attempt at creativity. However, the questionable selfie has been transmitted, which again, leaves her relying on the receiver's integrity.

Question#2 - **Encountering personal fundraising in the work place**

Correct Answer: **C** - Jana should choose the months that she wants to participate in purchasing items from fundraisers, and make this known to all in the office. With this choice, Jana exercises all the abilities in our toolkit. (20pts)

Commentary : Choice C in Jana's case is the best answer.

- ✓ Critical Thinking: Jana, although not in favor of childrens' fundraising in the work place, realizes this is condoned by management. She also takes note of her status as a new employee.
- ✓ Emotional Intelligence: Jana realizes she is working in a family oriented environment, and even though she is single, and has no children, she understands the need to forge a good working relationship with her co-workers, and establish herself as a team player.

✓ Flexibility: Although Jana would rather not participate, she finds a compromise that she can accept.

✓ Creativity : Jana creates a way to participate, that is made known. The office employees know her position / rule for participating in fund raisers. (i.e.: I only participate in the months of Feb., May, September, and December)

Choice B: Jana should buy items from the children in management (15pts)

A response of B shows both critical thinking and flexibility.

- Critical Thinking: Jana understands that it might not be to her advantage to completely avoid the fundraisers, or to say anything negative regarding them, since management approves of the practice, and they are involved as well. However if Jana had practiced emotional intelligence, she would have also considered how other employees felt about her action.

- Flexibility: Although Jana would rather not participate, she is flexible and compromises in a way that does not highlight her feelings with management.

Choice A: To be fair, Jana should try to buy something from each fundraiser. (10pts)

This choice shows:

- Emotional Intelligence: In attempting to be fair, Jana tries to 'spread the love'. However she is not thinking critically – considering how this choice could affect her finances.

Choice D: Jana should not participate in the purchasing of item for fundraising, and she should let her feelings regarding the practice be known to those in the office (5pts)

This choice does not use any of our toolkit abilities.

- Emotional Intelligence is lacking: Jana's open disapproval of the fundraising could potentially cause some alienation, hurt feelings, and a sense among her team members that she is not a team player.

- Critical Thinking in also lacking: If Jana chose this approach, she would not have considered the short and long-range impacts to her working relationship with her co-workers.

- Flexibility is missing too: With this approach, Jana appears rigid and not open to the dynamics of being a team player.

Question #3 - **Dealing with pungent fragrances in the work place**

Correct Answer: D - Report the issue to her boss. (20pts)

Commentary: Choice D shows three of the four abilities in play:

- ✓ Critical Thinking: Sandra understands the importance of keeping a positive working relationship in a small office setting. She logically considers the effects of bringing this problem to the forefront with her co-worker since her well-intentions could result in a negative confrontation.

✓ Emotional Intelligence: Sandra would not want to embarrass her co-worker by confronting her head-on.

✓ Creativity: Sandra is able to address the problem without fear of a negative confrontation, or embarrassing her co-worker, thus preserving their positive working relationship.

Choice A. Keep the windows and doors open (10pts)

This choice shows creativity and flexibility but not critical thinking and emotional intelligence.

- Creativity – By devising a solution to minimize the odor of the fragrance.
- Flexibility - By showing her willingness to find a way to address the problem without affecting the working relationship with her co-worker.

If Sandra had used her critical thinking skills, she would have considered how her solution might be flawed. Thinking ahead Sandra could have considered what her choice would mean in the winter time when it is very cold or raining. Would keeping the windows and doors open be a viable solution? Probably not. Emotional intelligence is also lacking. The other co-worker might not want to keep the doors and windows open. It could compromise privacy, and or increase the noise level.

Choice B: Politely and privately mention to her co-worker that her fragrance presents a problem (15pts)

This approach shows:

- Emotional intelligence - By addressing the issue politely and privately. It also shows empathy for the feelings of her co-worker.
- Creativity - There is a solution crafted to address the issue. But this choice lacks critical thinking and flexibility: What will the consequence of this conversation elicit? And how could this affect the working relationship between the two women going forth?

Choice C : Grin and bear it. (5pts)

This answer --to grin and bear it-- contains only one of our toolkit abilities - flexibility

- Flexibility: Sandra is willing to be flexible enough to endure the problem to avoid what could become a confrontational and or embarrassing scene that could potentially affect their working relationship. There is no critical thinking or creativity used to come up with a plan to solve the problem. And there is no display of emotional intelligence. Sandra is resigning herself to literally going to work every day and hating the air she breathes.

Question #4 - **Using social media prudently**

Correct Answer: C Beware of modern technology. Temporarily discontinue technology that allows access to the entrance of Sean's home when he is away for an extended amount of time <u>and</u>

Limit the information Sean posts on-line regarding his whereabouts, especially when he will be away for an extended amount of time. (20pts)

Commentary: Answer C exercises all four skills.

✓ Critical Thinking: Sean concludes that he may have to share some of the responsibility for his break-ins.

✓ Emotional Intelligence: Although Sean enjoys sharing his treasured experiences, he realizes there are times when best is less.

✓ Flexibiliy and Creativity: Sean is willing to alter his on-line behavior, and he devises a plan that hopefully will help to deter any additional home break-ins while he is on vacation.

Choice A: Beware of modern technology. Temporarily discontinue technology that allows access to the entrance of Sean's home when he is away for an extended amount of time (10pts)

Both creativity and critical thinking are evident in this choice.

• Creativity: Comes into play when a plan is crafted that addresses part of the problem - access into the home, but does not address the fact that Sean still makes himself vulnerable by disclosing via social media that he is away from home (showing an absence of emotional intelligence).

• Critical thinking: Also evident. Sean examines the facts, and realizes these break-ins are happening while he is on vacation. He considers the possibility that he may have made the break-ins easier.

Choice B: Limit the information he posts on-line regarding his whereabouts, especially when he will be away for an extended amount of time (15pts)

Like choice C (the correct answer), choice B contains all four skills. If it were not for the fact that Sean felt his technology could also be a factor in the break-ins, this answer would have been the correct answer. However, since both A and B were possible factors, C covers both.

Choice D: Limit the amount of vacation photos he posts on-line (5pts)

This choice only has value if Sean is willing to post his photos after-the-fact, and not when he is still on vacation.

Question #5 **Follow me following you**

Correct Answer: A Take only a small amount from each tray containing the food she desires. (20pts)

A, is the best choice because it contains the entire toolkit: critical thinking, emotional intelligence, flexibility, and creativity.

- ✓ Critical Thinking; Choice A shows critical thinking. Allesse wants to get enough to eat, but she realizes there is a good chance that there will not be enough food for some of the guest following her in line.
- ✓ Emotional Intelligence: Allesse uses her emotional intelligence when she shows her concern, and is considerate of those behind her. She is probably imagining how she would feel if she were at the end of the line, and there was little or no food left.
- ✓ Flexibility: Allesse is willing to forgo her desire to eat as much as she would prefer in order to accommodate those behind her.
- ✓ Creativity: Allesse devises a plan that she believes will take into consideration those following her. And hopefully others will follow her lead.

Choice B: (10pts) Fill her plate with the items from the trays that are not almost empty

This choice shows some:

- Critical thinking,- Allesse anticipates that there is a potential issue - a possible food shortage.

Choice B also shows some degree of :

- Flexibility, and creativity. However it is not enough to consider the possibility that her choice might mean the beginning of a shortage in the remaining trays that were not yet empty or almost empty. And for this reason, emotional intelligence is lacking.

Choice C: (15pts) Refrain from taking items from the trays that are almost empty.

- Like choice A, choice C contains use all of the skills; critical thinking, emotional intelligence, flexibility, and creativity. However, depending on how many trays were almost empty, Allesse could still find herself with only a couple of items on her plate. And let us not forget, Allesse is hungry. Although she wants to be considerate of those behind her, her generosity should not go so far as to guarantee she will be hungry throughout the remainder of the reception.

Choice D: (5pts) Notify the serving staff that there is not enough food

- Although choice D shows some creativity in finding a solution, the solution is one that is devoid of critical thinking, emotional intelligence, and flexibility. Using critical thinking, it is reasonable to believe that one would consider the awkwardness of approaching the food staff on behalf of the host. Emotional intelligence is not evident either; Speaking to the food staff, as a guest, could embarrass the host. There is also the potential of fracturing the relationship between the host and outspoken guest. And there is no evidence of a willingness on Allesse's part to alter her behavior.

Question #6: **Facing the weapon of mass distraction**

Correct Answer: D

Choice D, which combines A and C shows all four abilities. Cary should have said "Excuse me" before taking the call. Also Cary should have asked the caller if she could call her back. (20 pts)

✓ Critical Thinking: Cary realizes she has a dilemma and she wants to be courteous to both Patti and the caller. She also understands the importance of 'being in the present.'

✓ Emotional Intelligence: Aware that it would be rude to abruptly discontinue her conversation with Patti, Cary is courteous and excuses herself so that she can acknowledge the caller.

✓ Flexibility: Cary understands she must quickly adjust to the demands of the moment.

✓ Creativity: Instead of choosing one over the other, Cary creates a solution that accommodates both Patti and the caller – show respect and courtesy to both.

Choice A: (5 pts) Cary should have said "Excuse me" before answering the phone. There is some:

Emotional intelligence shown in this choice. At least Cary says, "Excuse me," but Cary still ignores Patti for far too long. If Cary had employed critical thinking, she would have taken into account the fact that there are two individuals to consider in this scenario. Cary does not adequately acknowledge the presence of Patti. Additionally Cary is not flexible. She reacts to her immediate impulse to not only answer the call but also continues a conversation with the caller, ignoring Patti.

There is no plan to take in account both people – no evidence of creativity or flexibility.

Choice B: (10 pts) Cary should have let the call go to voice-mail

Choice B doesn't take the caller into consideration. This option shows a lack of critical thinking. However it does show some evidence of:

- Emotional Intelligence: Although Cary acknowledges Patti's presence, there is no evidence of emotional intelligence rendered toward the caller. Failure to answer the call leaves the caller 'hanging' unnecessarily. Suppose the call is an emergency?
- Flexibility and Creativity: Cary shows some creativity and flexibility by letting the call go to voice-mail. However this is not an adequate plan. This choice does not address the entire scenario; the caller is still ignored.

Choice C: (15 pts) Cary should have asked the caller if she could call her back.

Like Choice B (see below), this choice takes into consideration only one part of this issue. It does however show evidence of:

- ✓ Critical Thinking: Because Cary keeps the call brief, she shows that she can think critically.
- ✓ Emotional Intelligence: She is considerate of Patti's time but not excusing herself to Patti prior to taking the call may make Patti feel like she is invisible.
- ✓ Flexibility: Cary shows flexibility by being willing to delay the phone call.

Question #7 – Facing the snail

Correct Answer: D Ron should send invitations by snail mail. He can also post the invitation on Facebook, and send a mass e-mail. (20pts)

Choice D. Contains all four of the skills

✓ Critical Thinking: Ron logically thinks through the process, and understands he needs a plan that will assure all his intended guests receive the invitation.

✓ Emotional Intelligence: Ron does not want to take the chance of anyone being excluded, simply because they did not get the invitation. This could potentially result in hurt feelings or worse.

✓ Flexibility: Ron is willing to go beyond what would be his preferred mode of sending invitations, to insure all are aware of the event.

✓ Creativity: Ron devises a plan that addresses a variety of the various modes of dispersing information, since he is not aware of exactly who has what type of on-line accounts.

Choice A: (5pts) Ron should post his reunion invitation on Facebook, and instruct the Facebook members to spread the word to those who do not have Facebook accounts.

This choice does not show any of the abilities in our toolkit.

- Critical Thinking: What happens if those on Facebook do not spread the word, or suppose someone does not have a computer or smart phone? Or perhaps an e-mail goes to 'junk mail', and is missed. Not critically-thinking-through these questions can produce negative unintended consequences. .

- Emotional Intelligence: Likewise, it shows no emotional intelligence. Those who are not on Facebook are likely not to get the invitation. How are they going to feel when they miss the event? And what does this say for Ron, the organizer?

- Creativity and Flexibility: Neither of these are exercised. Ron has chosen one way of dispersing the information, even though he is aware of the fact that there are probably some intended guests who are not on Facebook.

Choice B: (10pts) Ron should make phone calls to invite the guests

Choice B shows some emotional intelligence. Ron is going to attempt to speak to each person, so he has taken into consideration the possibility that all intended guest may not be 'on-line.' However, with this option he doesn't practice flexibility, creativity, nor critical thinking. In today's world of easy-to-access communication options, it is unreasonable not to use multiple methods to share information. What if the person does not answer the phone, or their mailbox is full? This would necessitate multiple phone calls, which is unreasonable when the list is extensive .

Choice C: (15pts) Ron should use an e-mail based application to send to his guest, since more of his guests might have e-mail than Facebook

Choice C illustrates the use of some critical thinking. Ron has taken into consideration that there are probably more intended guest with e-mail accounts than Facebook accounts. However this is another example of a single faceted approach that potentially could result in the exclusion of some intended guest. Again, what happens if an e-mail goes to 'junk', or accidently gets deleted? Since these possibilities are not considered, there is a lack of emotional intelligence, flexibility and creativity. Being flexible means the willingness to move or go beyond your preferences.

Question #8 – **The photographer wears many hats**

Correct Answer: C   He should ask the person standing behind Jamal to move to a different location. (20pts)

Choice C includes all four of our toolkit's abilities.

✓ Critical Thinking: The photographer perceives a problem when Jamal refuses to take off his hat. He uses his critical thinking skills, to make a quick analysis of the situation, to determine what will be an acceptable response to Jamal's refusal to remove his hat.

✓ Emotional Intelligence: The photographer may not know Jamal's issue with taking off his hat, but he uses his emotional intelligence, and avoids putting Jamal 'on the spot', so to speak.

✓ Flexibility: The photographer shows flexibility. He retreats from his request, and decides not to make an issue of Jamal's hat

✓ Creativity: Requesting the person behind Jamal to move is a creative way to get his desired result without causing a possible confrontation or embarrassment.

Choice A: (5pts) He should not take the picture until Jamal removes his hat

This choice shows none of our toolkit's abilities. It is lacking critical thinking, because refusing to take the picture until Jamal takes off his hat lends itself to a myriad of potential negative reactions - from Jamal, and possibly others.

• Emotional intelligence is not being used. The photographer fails to consider the possibility that Jamal may have a very good reason for not wanting to comply with his request. Perhaps his hair was not combed? If his hair was long / Afro-style, once he took his hat off -his hair would likely be in the shape of the hat, until he had time to comb it. This would likely not be a desirable look for a photo.

• Flexibility and creativity are also absent in this choice. There are no other options offered. This shows no flexibility, and a lack of creativity to come up with a solution.

Choice B: (10pts) He should ask Jamal to move to another location in the picture.

Choice B shows limited flexibility but not critical thinking, emotional intelligence, or creativity abilities.

• Critical Thinking: The photographer would not be critically-thinking since there is a definite possibility of a confrontation with this choice. There is already one request that has garnered a refusal, now the photographer would be setting himself up for yet another refusal; Jamal might refuse to move!!

- Emotional Intelligence: In this choice, there is little evidence of emotional intelligence. Asking Jamal to move could back him into a corner –triggering a power struggle or worse.
- Flexibility: There is some evidence of flexibility. The photographer is willing to allow Jamal to keep his hat on.
- Creativity: The creativity is minimal. The solution the photographer devises is one that could potentially lead to conflict.

Choice D: (15pts) He should simply proceed with the picture and disregard Jamal's hat

Choice D shows some critical thinking, emotional intelligence, and flexibility, but lacks creativity.

- Critical thinking: In this choice, the photographer mentally assesses the problem, and determines by thinking critically that it is not going to be productive to insist that Jamal remove his hat. However he then has to accept the fact that the person behind Jamal will likely not be seen in the picture.
- Emotional Intelligence: The photographer shows he is emotionally intelligent because he understands the potential consequences of insisting Jamal remove his hat. He realizes this could become a problem for others in the picture as well - inciting potential power struggles. . There is, however, one thing that is not taken into consideration - the feeling of the person who would be blocked from appearing in the picture.
- Flexibility: The photographer shows flexibility by allowing Jamal to keep his hat on.
- Creativity: This is a good example where a touch of creativity helps the situation, if not the whole problem. The photographer solved the problem of the hat, but what about the person who will be missing in the photo?

Question #9 – **A cornucopia of food options**

Correct answer: B Plan a pot-luck, allowing each employee to sign up for entrees, appetizers, and dessert. (20pts)

Choice B contains all four of the abilities in our toolkit

- ✓ Critical Thinking: Justin examines his situation, and acknowledges the diversity of the office, and the need to try to be as accommodating to all as possible.
- ✓ Emotional Intelligence: Justin does not want any of his employees to feel slighted.
- ✓ Flexibility: Justin is willing to consider a different approach than the one taken in previous years.
- ✓ Creativity: Justin finds an alternate way of approaching his dilemma, which he believes will be more accommodating for all his employees' dietary needs. With each person bringing one dish, this approach provides the opportunity for his employees to sample foods unfamiliar to their palates.

Choice A: (15pts) Enlist the help of a caterer to develop a menu and prepare the food

Shows some emotional intelligence, flexibility, creativity and critical thinking.

- Critical Thinking: Justin realizes he has a diverse group , so he plans to hire someone to accommodate the group.
- Emotional Intelligence: Justin shows that he wants to be considerate of the dietary needs of his staff.
- Flexibility: Justin is not satisfied with "business as usual". He is willing to make changes.
- Creativity: Justin devises a plan that he believes will be accommodating to the dietary needs of the staff.

Choice C: (10pts) Provide several diverse menus, and allow the staff to vote on their preferred one

Choice C shows some flexibility, however, it does not exercise the other three abilities.

- Critical thinking: Choice C does not show adequate critical thinking skills: If this choice was thought through logically, Justin would have considered a number of factors that could actually sabotage his plan of accommodation and inclusion. What if some people failed to vote? With 20 people and 3-4 menus, a small group of 5 or 6 could potentially determine the menu, thus leaving the others stuck with a menu that 14 or more people might not favor.

- Emotional Intelligence: There is little or no emotional intelligence employed. Justin does not consider those who could potentially not be considered in a food choice. Will they want to attend?

- Flexibility: Justin's approach shows flexibility by presenting several menu choices. But this attempt could backfire if only a few of the staff vote in a choice that the majority reject.

Choice D: (5pts) Stick with the menu that was used the year before

Choice D does not exercise any of the abilities from our toolkit.

- Critical Thinking: Justin realizes last year's choice was not 'a hit' with his staff. Repeating this choice is void of the critical thinking process.

- Emotional Intelligence: This choice does not take into consideration how the staff would feel about Justin knowingly repeating a choice that was not favored. What does this say about him as a leader?

- Flexibility: Justin's unwillingness to change shows no flexibility.

- Creativity: With no change, and no flexibility, there is no creativity.

Question #10 – Guess which guest?

Correct Answer: A Sarah could forego lunch and meet her friend at the church after attending Tina's tea. Then go to dinner after the church event with her church friend. (20pts)

Choice A includes all four abilities:

✓ Critical Thinking: Sarah realizes by tapping into her critical thinking skills that she may have a problem attending both events.

✓ Emotion Intelligence: Sarah does not want to disappoint either of her friends, and does not want to favor one event over the other.

✓ Flexibility: Sarah shows she is flexible by finding a way to avoid disappointing either of her friends.

✓ Creativity: Sarah figures out a way to attend both events - if her church friend is willing to have dinner with her instead of lunch.

Choice B : (10pts) Sarah could choose to attend only one of the events.

Choice B shows some critical thinking and some flexibility; However it does not show emotional intelligence and creativity.

- Critical Thinking: Sarah has thought through her dilemma, and determined she cannot attend both events, which is her desire, without making some changes to the schedule.

- Flexibility: Sarah shows flexibility when she decides to attend only one of the events, even though her desire is to attend both.

- Emotional Intelligence: Sarah fails to use this element adequately. She does not take into consideration the feelings of the friend, whose invitation she must decline.

- Creativity: Sarah does not think far enough through her solution to determine that her solution does not garner her desired result - to attend both events.

Choice C: In order to avoid a negative response, Sarah and her church friend could forego lunch, and attend Tina's tea, then attend the church event. (5pts)

This choice shows only some flexibility.

- Emotional Intelligence: Sarah does not consider Tina's feelings. How will Tina feel about an extra guest? What will Tina do if she cannot accommodate an additional person? Will this affect the relationship between Tina and Sarah?

- Flexibility: Sarah is willing to make some adjustment to accomplishing her goal of attending both events. However, her plan lacks critical thinking and creativity. Sarah's choice does not consider the position this puts Tina in - accommodating an extra guest.

Choice D: Sarah could call Tina, and ask if it would be acceptable to bring her church friend with her to the tea, then attend the church event. (15pts)

Choice D shows critical thinking, emotional intelligence, and some flexibility.

- Critical Thinking: Sarah has determined that there is a need to make some adjustments in order to be able to attend both events.
- Emotional Intelligence: Sarah takes into consideration the position she might be putting Tina into by inviting a guest to her tea unannounced, so she calls Tina in advance and asks permission to bring her church friend.
- Flexibility: Tina shows some flexibility by trying to adjust her schedule so that she can attend both events.
- Creativity: Choice D, unfortunately, does not show creativity. It does not take into consideration that Tina might resist accommodating an extra guest. What's the backup plan?

Scoring assessment

If you scored:

185 -200   You are 'culturally-tuned-in'! Like more challenges? Read our 'Culturally-Challenging' Scenarios chapter and see if you agree with our conclusions. You also might enjoy checking out our Resources section for a variety of books, videos and podcasts that delve deeper into the topics covered in this book.

155 – 180   You are well underway to being 'culturally-tuned-in.' Fine-tune your toolkit chops by reading our 'Culturally-Challenging' Scenarios chapter.

105 – 150   You have a sense of what it takes to be 'culturally-tuned-in.' But practice is key. Read our Toolkit and 'Culturally-Challenging' Scenarios chapters to deepen your understanding of how practicing these skills can really be a game changer' for optimizing positive outcomes in your life.

50 – 100   You are to be commended for reading so far. These concepts – our cultural toolkit of skills – may be new territory for you to consider. Keep the faith and continue to read the rest of our book where we describe further the benefits of understanding and practicing these skills.

Chapter 3

Life's Equation

My name is Connie Payne and I am the co-author of *The Don't Get Me Started! Toolkit*.

Some of the most rewarding moments of my life were spent teaching my favorite classroom subject: math. Ironically, as a student, I never particularly cared for math. This dichotomy remained a mystery for a number of years. Thankfully, a few years into my teaching career, I had an epiphany, and the answer became crystal clear. It was not so much the process of working with numbers that intrigued me -it was the orderly process of problem solving.

The Beauty of an Orderly Process

Unlike other subjects where opinions, conjecture, and exceptions abound, math requires critical thinking that follows an orderly process. This process ultimately yields either a right or wrong answer. There are no in-betweens. A perfect example of this process is the equation. To solve an equation, there is an order of operation that must be followed. To help the students remember the order, I used this tool: **P**lease **E**xcuse **M**y **D**ear **A**unt **S**ally. The first letter of each word reminds the student of the operation to use; P, parentheses, E, exponents, M, multiplication, D, division, A, addition, and S, subtraction.

When students contemplate an equation that appears as long as a complex sentence, their natural tendency is to perceive it as difficult. However, this perception can be altered once they discover that the problem can be solved by following pre-defined ordered steps. Finding 'X', then becomes more like solving a familiar puzzle. The sense of satisfaction and accomplishment my students expressed when they were able to break down an equation to a few simple steps gave me great satisfaction.

Life Mimics an Equation

Watching my students logically move through this process precipitated the question: Could this process be applied outside of the realm of mathematics, and if so how? I came to the realization that life very closely mimics an equation. The life situations and problems we face on a daily basis often resemble very long and seemingly difficult equations. Often when we focus on our problems and situations in their entirety, they may seem overwhelming and unsolvable. However, if we apply an order of operation process, focusing on one step at a time, little by little, the expected outcome emerges.

Let's explore how you can apply this approach to practicing our 'culturally tuned- in' toolkit of skills.

Isolating the parenthesis:

STEP 1. Critical Thinking: In this step you recognize the need to address an issue, and to consider how it can be approached.

Dealing with the exponents:

STEP 2. Emotional Intelligence: When considering an issue, you should always attempt to consider how the desired goal can be reached with minimal conflict, and with a sense of compassion and consideration for all involved.

Completing the equation:

STEP 3. Flexibility: This step enables you to explore various ways of addressing the issue: Compromise is often required to solve an issue.

STEP 4. Creativity: This step invites you to think outside of the box when necessary. Consider ways that might address as many facets of the issue as possible; the desired outcome is to approach and address every facet of the situation.

Following this process may seem like an arduous task to process and practice daily, and possibly multiple times each day - especially when you are required to respond to situations in a matter of seconds. But truth be known, most of us already follow the process to some degree. Our goal in writing this book is to bring conscious awareness to the process, and to suggest tips on how you can keep refining the process.

Chapter 4

The Culturally-Tuned-In Toolkit

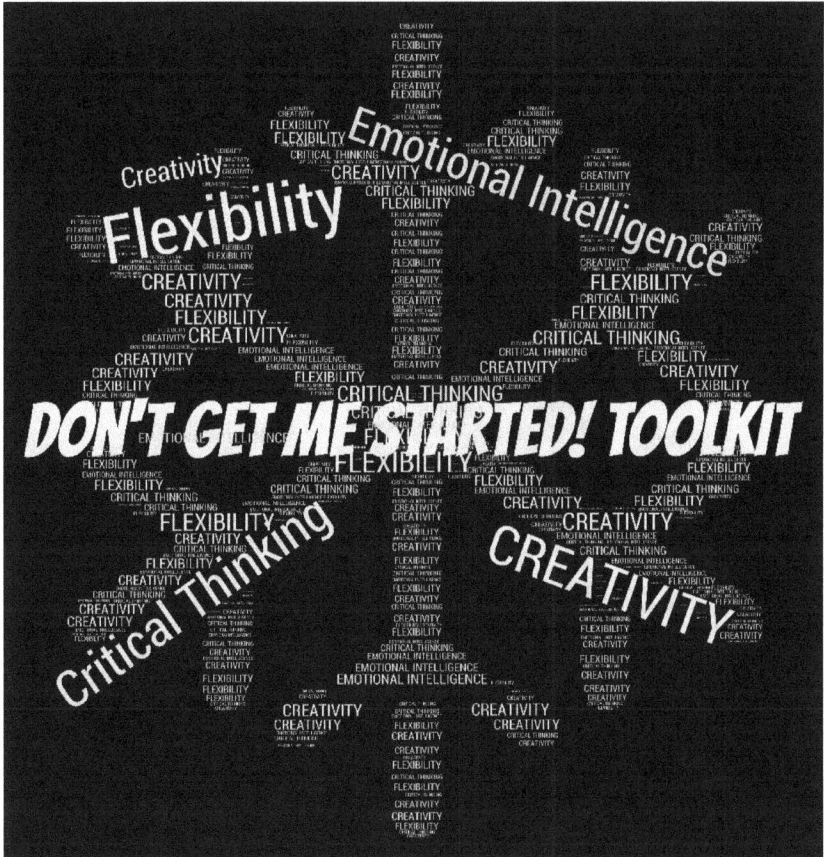

In our Cultural IQ Test chapter we talk about how exercising our toolkit skills (emotional intelligence, critical thinking, flexibility and creativity) helps you make informed choices that can reduce conflict, save face and find solutions that are win-win rather than win-lose or lose-lose.

Now let's look closer at each of these skills so that you will begin to recognize them in action.

The Skills

EMOTIONAL INTELLIGENCE

"I've learned that people will forget what you said, people will forget what you did, but people will never forget how you made them feel."

Maya Angelou

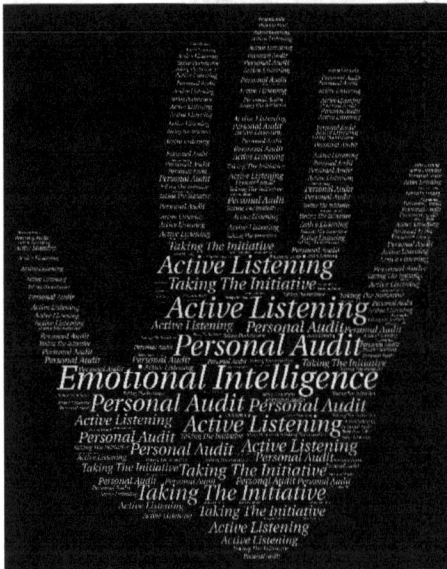

You know them when you meet them. When it comes to diffusing a potentially explosive situation at work, or just helping guests mingle at a party, people who are endowed with emotional intelligence seem to have the inside track about what to say and when to say it. It may even seem that they are born with magical skills. But truth to tell, this vitally important skill can be learned and like anything else, refined with practice.

Psychologists generally agree that emotionally intelligent people (EI,

54

for short) share the following traits:

1) They are aware of their own emotions and those of others
2) They understand the effects that their emotions have on other people
3) They regulate their own emotions for maximum benefits

They are aware of their own emotions and those of others

Emotions are like a swift-running current that flows through our bodies. Like most folks, the emotions of EI people run the full gamut of anger, sadness, joy, etc. The difference is that EI people have a built-in emotion detector that monitors this flow. And when, like most folks, they experience days when they feel especially vulnerable, EI people are able to set boundaries and assert themselves in a way that protects their sense of value without compromising others.

Revisiting our test questions:

Let's rewind for a minute and go back to our first quiz question: (A Case of Over-Sharing.)

Rhoda's middle school classmate dares her to take a very revealing 'selfie' and post it on Instagram. What should she do?

Let's imagine that Rhoda is normally a self-confident young woman. But on this day she is feeling a bit down and more vulnerable to suggestions that might offer to boost her spirits. Invoking her emotional intelligence, Rhoda, before consenting to take that selfie, would run a self-check of her feelings. And she would note that her vulnerable state is masking her better judgement – her self-knowledge that differentiates between the type of actions that truly build her confidence and those that threaten to undermine it.

They understand the effects that their emotions have on other people

Call it empathy mixed with wisdom. EI people tend to learn quickly from their mistakes —especially when their mistakes may inadvertently or deliberately cause others pain, embarrassment or grief.

<u>Revisiting our test questions:</u>

Let's return to our second quiz question: (Personal Fundraising in the Workplace.)

Jana is single and subject to constant fund-raising solicitations from her peers. She is searching for a way to feel like a team player but not bust her wallet in the process of doing so. What should Jana do?

Practicing her emotional intelligence, Jana knows that she enjoys the benefits of being perceived as a 'team player.' She also knows that she would feel resentful if she decided to say yes to each request for money. Her decision to explain how she will contribute lets her workers know that she wants to 'belong' and that she wants to be fair in the way she participates in their fundraising.

They regulate their own emotions for maximum benefits

We live in a world where instantaneous reactions are not only expected, but also encouraged, even when others are adversely affected. EI people, since they are constantly auditing their emotions, tend to resist reacting prematurely. They are the ones, in difficult situations, who are often calm - even when those around them have caved into destructive behavior.

<u>Revisiting our test questions:</u>

Let's return to Question#3 (Pungent Fragrances)

Sandra works in an office where one of her fellow workers wears perfume. The scent is so strong, it can be smelled throughout the entire office. This has made working very uncomfortable for Sandra. What should Sandra do?

Many people have experienced this issue in their workplaces. Unfortunately many of these people resort to catty remarks or other behavior that makes the situation much more stressful than it should. By referring this issue to her boss, Sandra avoids the 'personal' aspect of it. Instead of confronting the offending worker directly, Sandra uses the emotional intelligent approach – thus helping save face for her coworker as well as herself.

Habits that Nurture Emotional Intelligence

There are many ways you can help develop your emotional intelligence. Here are just a few:

1) Learn how to become an 'active listener.'

   Most people tend to think they are 'good listeners'. But if they were to try such 'listening' tests as given in the book, *What You Don't Know About Listening*[7] they might be surprised to discover that there is a big difference between passive and active listening. This book also does a very good job of describing the big payoff that 'active listeners' gain from practicing this skill.

2) Practice maintaining perspective regarding daily events in your life. *"Don't sweat the small stuff"*[8] says Richard Carlson, stress consultant and author of the book of the same name. "When you learn the habit of responding to life with more ease, problems that seemed 'insurmountable' will begin to seem more manageable" says Carlson.

---

[7] Jon F. White, and Alexandra Taketa, <u>What You Don't Know About Listening</u> (Could Fill A Book). (Amazon.com, 2014)

[8] Richard Carlson, <u>Don't Sweat the Small Stuff</u>, (Hachette Books, 1996)

3) Value the ability to empathize. In Chapter 5 of his best-selling book, *The 7 Habits of Highly Effective People,*[9] author Steven Covey stresses that it is more important that we 'seek first to understand and then, to be understood.' "When you listen with empathy to another person, you give that person psychological air" says Covey. "And after that vital need is met, you can then focus on influencing or problem solving."

CRITICAL THINKING

"It is the mark of an educated mind to be able to entertain a thought without accepting it"------Aristotle

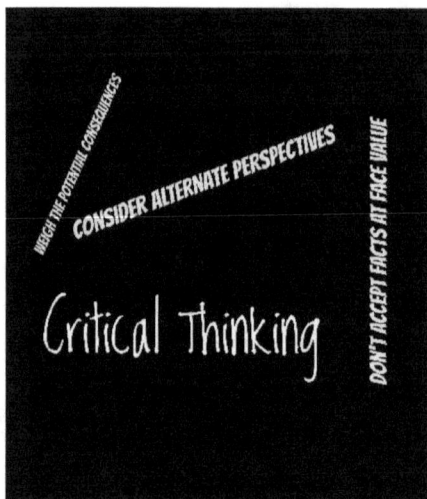

In our Life's Equation chapter, my co-author Connie Payne shares her insights, gleaned from a long teaching career. Now I, Patricia Kutza, would also like to share some learnings.

One of my favorite classes at San Francisco State's School of Broadcasting focused on an examination of the impact of media in our culture. This was the pre-Internet era and the focus was not on social media as it would most certainly be today. It was on the power and influence of the traditional broadcasting media platforms of that time: radio, television and cinema. My teacher's goal was to help us think critically about these platforms – analyzing them from political, economic and cultural perspectives. Her approach reaped big dividends for me – It has helped me as a journalist to appreciate the importance of analyzing and synthesizing information with a critical mindset– information culled from asking the kinds of questions to

---

[9] Steven Covey, The 7 Habits of Highly Effective People, (New York, Simon and Schuster, Anniversary edition, 2013)

myself and those I interviewed that are based on being aware of my own personal bias and often unconscious assumptions.

Critical thinking is an acquired skill and not just the province of journalists. Many job recruiters today state that it is a skill highly valued by employers in practically every job title and in every market category. And this fact has not gone un-noticed in K-12 education[10] where teachers are advocating that these skills be taught way before kids are eligible for employment.

Critical thinkers come in all sizes, ages and nationalities. They tend to share the following traits:

1. They tend to not accept facts at face value.
2. They tend to consider alternate perspectives, even when some of them clash with their own assumptions and bias.
3. They tend to think and weigh the potential consequences of their thoughts and decisions.

Let's go back to our test questions, once again, and see how the application of critical thinking plays such an important part in being 'culturally-tuned-in.

They tend to not accept facts at face value

Remember Justin's challenge? (Question 9 – A Cornucopia of Food Options)

Justin, the group supervisor of an office of approximately 20 employees, is responsible for planning the companies Christmas Party. He wants to improve upon last year's some- what unpopular choice of assorted sandwiches, fruit, and cookies. However, upon some investigating of his staff, he discovers the planning would be much more difficult than he had anticipated. Justin finds that his staff consists of five different ethnic groups, two vegans, three vegetarians, a diabetic, and one lactose intolerant employee. How should Justin approach this dilemma

---

[10] Criticalthinking.org: A-professional-development-model-for-k-12-schools-critical-thinking-as-the-key-to-substantive-learning

Justin could have made a quick assessment of last year's menu, deciding to make a few tweaks to it - based on his own assumptions (and perhaps his own food preferences). Instead he took the extra step and questioned his staff for their input. In doing so, he discovered that he needed to approach the planning from a new perspective: Considering the food and dietary preferences of his employees.

They tend to consider alternate perspectives, even when some of them clash with their own assumptions and bias.

What would you do in Ron's case? (Question 7 – Facing the Snail)

Ron volunteers to organize the next family reunion. His guest list is extensive, spanning three generations of family members. Ron's a big Facebook fan and many of his family members have Facebook accounts. What is the best way for Ron to disperse the invitations?

There was a time when folks communicated either face-to-face or via the written word. Nowadays they can pretty much cherry-pick their mode of communicating, with a vast variety of modes to choose from --.such as Skype, texting, online chat, Instagram, Twitter, Facebook, etc. So the present challenge is to be able to dovetail one's own communication preferences with those of others.

Using critical thinking, Ron would consider the fact that his own communication preference – Facebook – is not shared by everyone on his invitation list. He searches for the most inclusive way to spread the news

They tend to think and weigh the potential consequences of their thoughts and decisions

If you were the photographer at this group shoot, what would you do? (Question 8 – The Photographer Wears Many Hats)

Jamal, a young African- American, is asked to take his hat off for a group photo. Jamal is told it is blocking the face of the person behind him. Jamal refuses to remove his hat.

Photography can be tricky business – especially when everyone being photographed wants to be represented in their most favorable light. But the best of photographers know that making the subjects feel comfortable is just as important as framing the shot. In this scenario, a smart photographer weighs the options (who can move where within the frame) and resists imposing his will – eg demanding that Jamal take off his hat. By doing so, he avoids unnecessary confrontation, keeping the vibe upbeat

Habits that Support and Encourage Critical Thinking

1) Sharpen your questioning skills

Much emphasis is made about the importance of asking well-crafted questions during a job interview. Yet little mention is made of the fact that critically-constructed questions not only offer interviewers the chance to receive more valuable information about the people they interview. Thoughtfully-crafted questions also reflect well on both the interviewer and interviewee's capacity to leverage their critical thinking skills to their advantage.

As Andrew Sobel says in his book *Power Questions*[11], thought-provoking questions not only give power to your conversations. They also impart other important benefits – like giving power to the other person to talk about what's important to them. It's not about you grabbing more power for yourself but rather being perceived as a wise and thoughtful person, he says.

2) Practice mediation

We live in a highly competitive world where the dynamics of sports - its win/lose structure – influence the way people interact with each other at work and at play as well as the way they chose to resolve their differences.

---

[11] Andrew Sobel, and Jerold Panas, <u>Power Questions: Build Relationships, Win New Business and Influence Others.</u> (New York: Wiley, 2012)

Mediation is an alternative method for resolving issues. It moves the focus away from dwelling on the 'right/wrong' perspective. Instead the parties who use mediation look for win-win solutions – trying a cooperative rather than adversarial approach.

FLEXIBILITY

"Notice that the stiffest tree is easily cracked while the bamboo survives by bending in the wind"------Bruce Lee

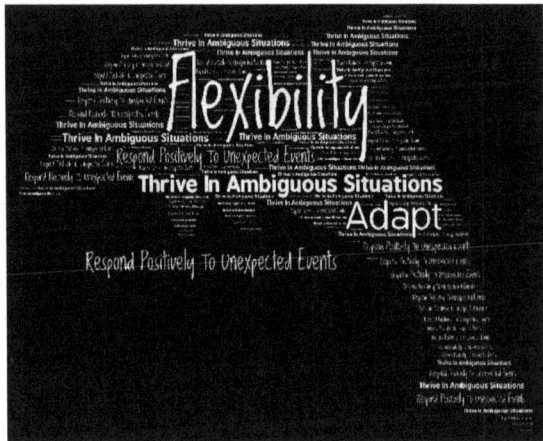

Bruce Lee is one of the most iconic figures of the twentieth century. With his highly celebrated blend of skill and flexibility, Lee elevated his martial arts technique to an art form. More than forty years after his untimely death, it is the flexibility of his mind as well as his body that many of his devotees still admire and remember.

Naysayers warn that persons with flexible attitudes are only pushovers. But they would do well to consider the biologist Charles Darwin's admonition that it is not the strongest nor most intelligent who survive, but the ones most responsive to change.

Like emotional intelligence and critical thinking, flexibility is an acquired skill. And in a highly competitive global economy, where the boundaries of opportunity are constantly shifting, workers who can quickly adapt to a variety of work environments are in high demand

Flexible people tend to share the following traits:

1) They are able to respond to unexpected events in a positive way.
2) They often positively adapt to situations that unfold differently from what they hoped or imagined.
3) They thrive in ambiguous situations where they can exercise their creativity by applying their emotional intelligence and critical thinking skills.

Let's return to our test questions. As we review some of the best answers, notice how often the skill of flexibility works hand-in-hand with critical thinking and emotional intelligence – reinforcing the skill-set necessary to becoming 'culturally tuned-in.

They are able to respond to unexpected events in a positive way

Remember Sarah's dilemma? (Question 10, - Multiple Invitations)

Sarah was invited to high tea by her friend Tina, however, Sarah had also agreed to go to lunch and attend a church function with another friend on the same day. The events were approximately two and a half hours apart. Sarah could attend both events, if she was mindful of the time factor of each. Sarah really wants to attend both. What would be the best approach to solving this dilemma?

Many events in life are outside our control. Sarah experiences this fact when she receives two invitations that are scheduled for the same time. She could take the path of least resistance and just accept one of the invites. Or she could also create a major faux pas by taking her uninvited church friend to the high tea. Instead Sarah finds a way to spend time with both friends – thus avoiding hurt feelings or other misunderstandings.

They often positively adapt to situations that unfold differently from what they hoped or imagined.

Consider Sean's situation: (Question 4, - Using Social Media Prudently)

Sean, a social media buff, broadcasts all over the Net in real time his whereabouts while on vacation from his home. He also brags about the technology he uses to control access to his home. Sean experiences a home break-in while on this vacation. In fact this is his second break-in while on vacation

Like many people who have embedded social media platforms into the very fabric of their lives, Sean is faced with balancing the private details of his life with his desire to share every part of it. Unfortunately this situation leaves him open to unforeseen and unintended consequences. Using his critical thinking skills Sean could connect the dotted lines and see a pattern of consequences to his online behavior. By exercising flexibility, he can adapt positively by not only being careful about what he shares but also when he shares it.

They thrive in ambiguous situations where they can exercise their creativity by applying their emotional intelligence and critical thinking skills

Let's revisit Jana's challenge: (Question 2, Personal Fundraising in the Workplace)

Jana, is single and a new employee at an accounting firm, where most of the employees are married and have children. Practically every month, there are multiple solicitations from the children of employees; management included. Jana feels this has gone beyond what is reasonable, and also feels it is unprofessional. She is searching for a way to feel like a team player but not bust her wallet in the process of doing so.

When Jana signed on with the accounting firm, most likely she was given their employee handbook, a 'bible' of sorts that outlines the company's rules and regulations regarding her performance on the job. Most likely what the handbook does not mention are the more intangible expectations, such as the way she interacts with her team members.

When faced with her situation, a team member who makes it a principle of never contributing to such solicitations might flaunt his rigid stance by remaining aloof or unapproachable. A 'flexible' Jana seeks an inclusive solution that shows her willingness to participate in the team ritual, but on her own terms.

Habits that Support and Encourage Flexibility

1) Whenever possible, experiment with 'rearranging' your daily routine. For example, if you always use the same route to drive home from the super-market, try using an alternate route.

2) Look for opportunities that take you out of your 'comfort zone.'

"We gain strength, and courage, and confidence by each experience in which we really stop to look fear in the face. You must do the things you think you cannot do." Eleanor Roosevelt once advised.

3) Periodically list your personal or professional goals. Then list at least five alternate ways of achieving them.

CREATIVITY

"Creativity is intelligence having fun" – Albert Einstein

Not too long ago, an all-points alert was broadcast across San Francisco when a man kidnaped a child. In his haste to escape, the kidnaper and his victim boarded a San Francisco bus. The bus driver, only minutes earlier having heard the alert that gave details about the physical appearance of the child, thought he recognized the child and his kidnaper when they boarded the bus.

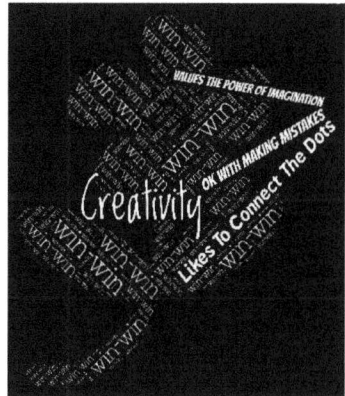

Not wanting to telegraph his discovery, the bus driver stopped the bus a short time after it departed from the bus stop. Using the pretense that he was searching for a lost back pack, the driver scanned each passenger seat as if he was looking for the back pack.

65

When he reached the kidnaper and the child, he did the same scan, except his purpose was to confirm that the little boy was wearing red shoes. When he confirmed that fact, he returned to the driver's seat and alerted authorities as soon as the kidnaper and child exited the bus. The kidnaper was soon apprehended and the child was freed

While some folks think that creativity is solely the gift of artists and performers, it is a fact that everyday people who don't even consider themselves artistically or theatrically inclined make creative decisions. Most likely they are inclined to do it often. The great dancer Twyla Tharp, known for her ground-breaking choreography says it succinctly: "Creativity is a habit and the best creativity is the result of good work habits."

Which leads us to adding creativity to our toolkit, alongside emotional intelligence, critical thinking and flexibility. By now we hope it is amply apparent that all of these four skills work in tandem, and honing anyone of these skills makes you predisposed to develop the others.

Creative people tend to share the following traits:

- Their desire to test their ideas is stronger than their fear of making mistakes
- They are attracted to opportunities where they can 'connect the dots.'
- They value the power of their imagination.

Let's return to some of our test questions to see how creative approaches often offer 'win-win' solutions.

Their desire to test their ideas is stronger than their fear of making mistakes

Reviewing Justin's challenge: (Question 9, A Cornucopia of Food Options)

Justin, the group supervisor of an office of approximately 20 employees, was responsible for planning the companies Christmas Party. He wanted to improve upon last year's some-what unpopular choice of assorted sandwiches, fruit, and cookies. However, upon some investigating of his staff, he discovered the planning would be much more difficult than he had anticipated. Justin found that his staff consisted of five different ethnic groups, two vegans, three vegetarians, a diabetic, and one lactose intolerant employee.

Justin could have hired a caterer, or even asked the staff to weigh in on a few menus. Instead he decided on an approach that had the potential to be very interesting or very dull – a potluck that depended on the imagination and interest of his employees. Since he made sure that all categories were covered, eg. Entrees, appetizers and desserts, Justin decreased the possibility that the dishes were skewed to any one category

They are attracted to opportunities where they can 'connect the dots.'

Remember Allesse? (Question 5, Follow Me Following You)

She's the one who attended a wedding reception, which included a buffet of a variety of food items. Allesse was standing toward the end of the buffet line. There were approximately 80 people in front of her and approximately 30 additional people behind her. As she approached the food, she noticed quite a few trays were almost empty.

Sometimes creativity means modelling 'sensible' behavior. Not knowing if the food trays would eventually be replenished for the two dozen plus people waiting behind her, Allesse could choose to take only a small amount of food from each tray that appealed to her. By doing so, she gets to eat what she likes. But she also signals to the folks in line behind her that she is aware that the food supply may be limited.

They value the power of their imagination

Let's take our hats off to insightful photographers! (QUESTION #8 – The photographer wears many hats).

By virtue of their trade, photographers are creative people. But they are more often called to practice their 'photographic' skills rather than those related to conflict resolution. In the optimal resolution to potential conflict, the photographer reaches into his imagination to search for a solution that promises a great shot but not at the expense of his subjects.

Habits that Support and Encourage Creativity

1) Practice creating open-ended questions (such as "What human language sounds closest to your dog's bark?"). At first blush this exercise may sound outlandish. But training your mind to consider the similarities between two seemingly disparate subjects can be a productive exercise.

   Looking for more practice? Try some of the 250 + 'brain-stretching' exercises featured in *Caffeine for the Creative Mind: 250 Exercises to Wake Up Your Brain*[12]

2) Periodically rearrange your work space or play space at home.

3) Try to capture the contents of your dream by writing, drawing or vocalizing them.

Assumptions and Best Practices

In the Introduction, we mentioned that our book's goal is to give you a toolkit – a set of abilities that you can use to successfully navigate this fast-paced and often confusing world we live in.

Every set of abilities comes with a belief system – assumptions that translate into a series of 'best practices.' Ours is no different.

---

[12] Stefan Mumaw, and Wendy Lee Oldfield, Caffeine for the Creative Mind: 250 Exercises to Wake Up Your Brain. (HOW Books, 2006)

Don't Gloss Over The Differences
Weigh Consequences Of Their Behavior
Consider Personal And Professional
Mindful Voicing Their Opinions
Sensitive To Personal Space
Understand The Similarities Among Cultures

Best Practices

Life Very Valuable Real Estate
Value Expressions Of Mutual Respect

In the bulleted sentences below, we share the best practices that we think 'culturally-tuned-in' folks continually adhere to – applying their abilities of critical thinking, emotional intelligence, creativity and flexibility to successfully met the challenges of living in these hectic, but exciting times.

- They are sensitive to the boundaries of personal space – their own and others
- They are mindful about how and when they voice their opinions
- They consider the details of their personal and professional life as very valuable real estate (less is more)
- They weigh the consequences of their behavior
- They seek to understand the similarities among cultures but don't gloss over the differences.
- They value expressions of mutual respect

In the next section, we review more scenarios - situations in your everyday lives that can test your common sense and ability to adapt to change. For short, we call them "Culturally-Challenged Scenarios." - Our goal is to demonstrate how applying our toolset of skills and best practices to these situations offers you new ways to assess such situations, and try alternate positive ways of responding.

Chapter 5

The Don't Get Me Started! Toolkit
Culturally-Challenged Scenarios

The Don't Get Me Started! Toolkit
Culturally-Challenged Scenarios

Modern day life can be so chaotic that it's easy to pine for easy solutions – quick magic that will help you make the best decisions.

We don't offer you magic. But we hope that you will be interested in taking a fresh look at situations that present similar challenges to some you may encounter in everyday life. As you consider options for handling them, notice how often the skills of critical thinking, emotional intelligence, creativity and flexibility work together to offer you win-win options.

The following scenarios are grouped by the major challenges we talk about earlier in this book:

- Rapid changes in technology
- Generational and ethnic differences
- Gender identity challenges
- Shifting personal boundaries in public spaces

RAPID CHANGES IN TECHNOLOGY

I DON'T STOP FOR SIGNS

Dan is waiting in his doctor's office reception area. At the sign-in desk, and in two other locations of the room, there are signs that inform patients that cell phone usage in the reception room is prohibited. Yet two of the five other people in the reception room are carrying on lengthy loud conversations on their cell phones. In addition to being annoyed, Dan feels very uncomfortable with some of what he is hearing, but does not know what to do.

What are his options?

TOOLKIT TO THE RESCUE

- **Critical Thinking**

Dan has not yet moved into critical thinking mode. He is uncertain of his options. In this particular case, Dan can opt to stay seated and do nothing, which would indicate his willingness to accept his discomfort. Or Don could consider what actions are in his control, possibly discovering one that may at least diminish his discomfort.

- **Emotional Intelligence**

If he considers confronting the cell phone users, Dan's emotional intelligence should prompt him to be wary of using this option. Any attempt to admonish the offenders could trigger a negative confrontation, and Dan understands that it is not his responsibility to enforce the rules of the business establishment.

- **Flexibility**

Instead of considering how to change the behavior of the offenders, Dan can opt to be flexible himself.

- **Creativity**

Dan could request that the receptionist call him on his cell phone when his doctor is ready for him. In the meantime, Dan can go elsewhere to wait.

TEACHABLE MOMENT

Society institutes rules governing our behavior for specific reasons. In a business setting, rules are established to insure a professional atmosphere. When the rules are not followed, it can have an adverse effect on the business.

Related Best Practices of 'Culturally-tuned-in' People:

- ✓ They value expressions of mutual respect.
- ✓ They consider the details of their personal life as valuable real estate.
- ✓ They are sensitive to the boundaries of personal space; their own and others.

WORDS TO THRIVE BY

"Rudeness is the weak man's imitation of strength." Christopher Hitchen

---

PAUSE BEFORE POSTING

Stephen lands a very coveted position in the security department for the upcoming Super Bowl. In his excitement, he announces his good fortune on Facebook, posting a picture of himself wearing his security badge.. (Stephen does not consider the fact that his security number is on the badge.) Two days later, his boss, seeing the post, informs him that he has breached his security contract. The position is re-assigned to someone else, and this coveted opportunity is lost.

How could have practicing our toolkit of abilities help Stephen avoid this mistake?

TOOLKIT TO THE RESCUE

- **Critical Thinking**

Stephen does not consider the fact that his security numbers are on his badge. As a security employee, this is a blunder that screams, "Lacking critical thinking!" Professional conduct is a requirement for all jobs and an important fact that all employees must consider even when they are not 'on the job', e.g. outside of their normal business hours.

- **Emotional Intelligence**

Stephen is a security professional. Prevention of security breaches is a large part of his job. He, more than most people, knows the prevalence of identity theft and misrepresentation. Likewise, on Face Book, all "Friends'" are not necessarily 100% "Friends." Stephen's excitement overshadows his sense of good judgement, and he lapses into "Friend Mode," throwing caution to the wind. Stephan should consider the fact that his responsibility to his employer supercedes his desire to share.

- **Flexibility**

While Stephen may regularly use social media to share news, he would do well to find alternate ways to connect that don't jeopardize his job. Perhaps texting, calling or emailing his friends, without using the photo, could suffice.

- **Creativity**

Using a stroke of creativity, Stephen could have made the tiny adjustment of either covering up the numbers on his badge prior to posting, or, posting a picture without the badge.

TEACHABLE MOMENT

Modern technology has increased our ability to instantaneously send and receive information. The "send" button is now synonymous with the town criers of old – anyone could be the potential recipient of the message. Therefore, it is imperative that any postings, including pictures, be scrutinized prior to pushing "send."

Related Best Practices of 'Culturally-tuned-in' People:

- ✓ They consider the details of their personal and professional life as very valuable real estate.
- ✓ They weigh the consequences of their behavior.

WORDS TO THRIVE BY

"A little of what you fancy does you good."   Proverb

DITCH THAT CELL

Al and Louise invite their extended family -parents, adult children, grandchildren, siblings with families, and a host of other relatives - to their annual Christmas dinner. Feeling frustrated during past family events where so much of their extended family was distracted by smart phone usage, Al and Louise decide to try a new approach.

This year, in an effort to promote more personal interaction, Al attempts to collect their guests' phones upon entrance. When two twenty-something relatives arrive and refuse to surrender their phones, Al is literally left holding the bag.

How did Al and Louise fall short of their well-intentioned goal?

TOOLKIT TO THE RESCUE

- **Critical Thinking**

  Al and Louise did not consider all of the potential effects of their decision – like the possibility of that someone would resist their demand – and what to do if this happened. Critical thinkers consider alternate perspectives - even when some clash with their own assumptions or bias.

- **Emotional Intelligence**

  By confronting their guests at the front door with this demand, Al and Louise not only unnecessarily put their guests on the spot. They also assume that none of their guests would need their phones for very valid reasons that they might not want to disclose to their hosts, Al and Louise.

- **Flexibility**

  Al could have greeted guests with a request rather than a demand – Asking guests to keep their phone usage to a minimum would have more likely been met with compliance than resistance.

- **Creativity**

Either-or solutions, like the one Al and Louise chose, often close the door on creativity. Here are some alternative win-win solutions that they could have considered: Designating a small area of their home for cell usage; Designating the dinner table as a cell-free zone; Noting their requests for minimum cell phone usage in their party invitations.

TEACHABLE MOMENT

For many people, cell phones serve a function greater than just a basic communication device. These devices have become appendages as important as any critical body parts. Rules of etiquette for dealing with this condition are still in flux. Folks who can rely on critical thinking, emotional intelligence, flexibility and creativity will have the toolkit necessary to make the best choices as our society evolves with this technology.

Related Best Practices of 'Culturally-tuned-in' People:

- ✓ They are mindful about where and when they voice their opinions.
- ✓ They value expressions of mutual respect.
- ✓ They weigh the consequences of their behavior

WORDS TO THRIVE BY:

"Any situation or offer should be considered from different angles." Sunday Adelaja

GENERATIONAL AND ETHNIC DIFFERENCES

STICKS, STONES AND WORDS DO HURT

Ashley and her husband are standing in a long line awaiting their turn to purchase theater tickets. In front of them is a group of teens: two boys and two girls. The teen's conversations are loud and riddled with the use of the "F" word, and the "N" word. Ashley, an African-American woman, is particularly outraged, but is uncertain of what to do. She wants to see the movie, but not at the expense of her dignity.

What are Ashley's options?

TOOLKIT TO THE RESCUE

- **Critical Thinking**

Ashley uses her critical thinking skill to identify the problem, and thoughtfully weighs her options – an important practice for critical thinkers.

- **Emotional Intelligence**

If Ashley taps into her emotional intelligence, she will likely conclude that confronting these teens is not a viable option. Why? Confrontation could possibly escalate the negative behavior because admonishing others publicly is rarely met with a graceful response.

- **Flexibility**

At this point, Ashley must determine just how flexible she wants to be. She could do nothing, and endure the teens for the length of time it takes to get to the ticket window. She can also leave or devise a plan that includes some form of middle ground.

- **Creativity**

Often the will to be creative reveals new options. Ashley and her husband could opt for the middle ground by deciding to go to the end of the line which, due to being outside, would likely be out of earshot of the teens' outburst.

TEACHABLE MOMENT

There are some situations that leave us with less than desirable options -This example being one of them. Confronting aggressive and or extreme behavior leaves the door open for negative unintended consequences.

Related Best Practices of 'Culturally-tuned-in' People:

- ✓ They are mindful about how and when to voice their opinion.
- ✓ They weigh the consequences of their behavior
- ✓ They value expressions of mutual respect.
- ✓ They are sensitive to the boundaries of personal space; their own and others

WORDS TO THRIVE BY

"Better safe than sorry" American Proverb

CRY BABIES

Will and Tina attend a very popular "R" rated movie. About 15minutes into the show, apparently the candy supply is cut-off from the whining child behind them. His whining makes following the dialogue extremely difficult. Despite turning around and giving several annoyed glances, this child continues to whine.

Will and Tina are at their wits end! What should they do?

TOOLKIT TO THE RESCUE

- • **Critical Thinking**

Tina and Will's annoyed glances indicate that their critical thinking wheels are in motion. They have tried a rather subtle tactic to avert the problem, but to no avail.

- • **Emotional Intelligence**

Being parents themselves, they empathize with the dilemma of the parent ("This parent is frustrated and needs help!") At this point, any verbal form of addressing the problem to the parent is out of the question. Besides, talking during the show is prohibited.

- **Flexibility**

So now what? Well this is when Will and Tina reach into their tool-set and pull out their habit of being flexible . Instead of expecting the frustrated mother to solve the problem, Will and Tina simply get up and find seats as far away from the whining child as possible.

- **Creativity**

The act of moving to another seat also sends a message to the parent without speaking a word.

TEACHABLE MOMENT

Whenever prudent and possible, solving a personal problem is the responsibility of those who are affected by the problem. We have little or no control over those who do not follow protocol or rules, but we do have the right and the power to adjust our behavior accordingly.

Related Best Practices of 'Culturally-tuned-in' People:

- ✓ They are sensitive to the boundaries of personal space, their own and others.
- ✓ They value expressions of mutual respect.
- ✓ They are mindful about how and when they voice their opinions.
- ✓ They weigh the consequences of their behavior

WORDS TO THRIVE BY

When the going gets tough, the tough get going.   American Proverb

BARKING UP THE WRONG TREE

Brent is a twenty-something owner of a loveable golden retriever. His dog often accompanies him in his travels, which can be anywhere from his dog-friendly workplace, a dog-friendly café, or a dog park to impromptu parties at his college friends' homes. On this occasion, Brent is invited to a barbecue where multi generations will mix. Since it is an outdoor event, he decides to bring his golden retriever along. Upon their arrival, they are greeted by a less than welcoming hostess, and a group of screaming children who are afraid of the dog. Brent apologizes for bringing his dog, but is still clueless as to who is really responsible for this mis-step.

How could practicing our culturally-tuned-in toolkit help Brent avoid this blunder?

TOOLKIT TO THE RESCUE

- **Critical Thinking**

Regarding invitations, many people still regard Emily Post's rules of party etiquette – that say only people invited by the host should attend - as the gold standard.. But Brent wouldn't need to know those fine details. Once he is aware of the children' reactions, his critical thinking skill should have alerted him about alternate perspectives that he didn't consider in advance.

- **Emotional intelligence**

While Brent may be accustomed to bringing his pet around people and places that are dog-friendly, it's still likely that Brent would have encountered previous situations where the presence of his dog was an issue. Using his emotional intelligence, he should have drawn upon those experiences, and concluded the presence of his dog might affect the dynamics of the event. While Brent enjoys the company of his pet, he still needs to be aware and considerate of the feelings of others.

- **Flexibility**

For this particular scenario, there are really only two choices: Take

81

the pet, or attend the party without the pet. Brent needs to understand that there will be times when it will not be appropriate to bring his pet along. However, in this case, the deed is done. So now what? Brent could take his dog home and return to the barbecue without him.

- **Creativity**

Would it have been creative of Brent to ask the hostess ahead of time if it would be acceptable to bring his pet? Please read the *Teachable Moment* that follows to see why this is not a viable option.

TEACHABLE MOMENT

According to Emily Post, "An invitation is extended to the people the hosts want to invite—and no one else."[13] Asking if you can bring someone else with you is a no-no. With this said, if it is unacceptable to ask permission to bring people, certainly the same should apply for a dog! Service animals are an exception to this rule because they are a lifeline for their owners and are exceptionally well-trained. Generally, in this case, the host /hostess should be made aware in advance of the need of the invited guest to have the service animal accompany them, thus giving he or her the latitude to respond with grace in advance.

Related Best Practices of 'Culturally-tuned-in' People:

- ✓ They are sensitive to the boundaries of personal space.
- ✓ They weigh the consequences of their behavior
- ✓ They value expressions of mutual respect

WORDS TO THRIVE BY

"Treat invitations like underwear. They are for your use only!" Connie Payne

---

[13] EmilyPost.com/Invitations - Etiquette

A HAIRY SITUATION

One of her work associates invites Kiana to a pool party. Kiana would love to attend, but she plans to get her hair straightened the day before. Kiana's hair (she is African-American) will become frizzy and kinky if she gets it wet. So she decides to go to the pool party, but will not bring a swimsuit -that way, she will have an excuse for not swimming. When she arrives, the hostess, Breanna, discovers that Kiana is without a swimsuit, so she offers to loan her one of hers. Kiana is standing with a group of friends when this offer is made. She is caught off guard, and is lost for words.

How can both Kiana and Breanna save face?

TOOLKIT TO THE RESCUE

- **Critical Thinking**

Kiana understands her dilemma. She doesn't want to get her hair wet and she formulates what she thinks is a viable solution so that she won't get her hair wet: She will go to the pool party without a swimsuit.

- **Emotional Intelligence**

Neither Kiana nor Breanna are fully tuned into their emotional intelligence. Kiana should not be surprised that her host would try to accommodate her arriving suit-less. Perhaps Breanna is thinking that Kiana forgot her swimsuit. Kiana should have expected Breanna at the very least, to make an inquiry. Breanna's emotional intelligence should have cautioned her about putting Kiana on the spot, so to speak, in the presence of others. Kiana's reason for arriving without a swimsuit could have been of an extremely personal nature, one that she might not want to share with a group of people. Therefore Breanna's inquiry, in the presence of others, was a breach of Kiana's privacy. Breanna would have showed her emotional intelligence by asking her in private.

- **Flexibility**

Kiana is aware that a swim party implies getting wet. If getting her hair wet is an issue, she could have declined the invitation, or been honest, and informed Breanna ahead of time that she would attend but not swim.

- **Creativity**

It is quite conceivable that Breanna is completely unaware of the dynamics of Black hair. Being honest with Breanna prior to the swim party would not only potentially avert the confrontation, but it could also help to bridge the gap of understanding regarding this particular cultural difference.

TEACHABLE MOMENT

The hair of those of African descent is uniquely different from the hair of most others. Any form of precipitation will cause it to become frizzy and or kinky. Modern conveniences such as chemical straighteners and flat irons straighten the hair. However, it is only temporary. The process of straightening the hair is time consuming and can be expensive; generally not worth a dip in the pool.

Related Best Practices of 'Culturally-tuned-in' People:

- ✓ They seek to understand the similarities among cultures, but do not gloss over the differences.
- ✓ They weigh the consequences of their behavior.

WORDS TO THRIVE BY

"To be forewarned is to be forearmed"   American Proverb

THE WHINE BUS

A ladies book club, which consists mainly of African American woman ranging in age from around 40-70, decide to take an excursion on the popular Wine Bus. During the trip, the women talk and laugh in what is later referred to by some in attendance as "too boisterous". A complaint is lodged, resulting in a warning from one of the bus' staff members: The ladies are told that they must lower their voices, or they could be asked to get off the bus.

When the group continues to laugh and talk louder than the bus staff deem acceptable, they are told to get off the bus at the next stop. The embarrassed and enraged women immediately broadcast their complaints on social media and these complaints quickly go viral. The consequences of the staff member's actions are far reaching. The negative press affects the popular Wine Bus brand, and the book club members also file a discrimination case.

What options did the Wine bus staff member neglect to consider?

TOOLKIT TO THE RESCUE

- **Critical Thinking**

Regardless of nationality, partaking in the consumption of spirits is bound to elicit conversation and laughter that might be louder than usual in many cases. A critical thinking employee should have anticipated this possibility and considered how to handle the situation in a non- confrontational manner.

- **Emotional Intelligence**

An emotionally-intelligent employee would understand that mixing alcohol and confrontation makes a very volatile cocktail.

- **Flexibility**

To paraphrase an oft-quoted wisdom: When the going gets tough, the tough find a way to bend. Perhaps engaging all the passengers in a prize-winning game would diffuse the situation.

- **Creativity**

Event providers, such as the Wine Bus, typically fund public relations departments that are well-versed in crisis communications. Offering complimentary wine to those who complain is a frequent gesture and could also have been tried.

TEACHABLE MOMENT

Discrimination is a serious charge that few companies can afford to weather, regardless of the outcome. In addition to the initial expenses that may or may not be recovered, the negative publicity could permanently damage the company's brand.

This definite lack of critical thinking, emotional intelligence, flexibility and creativity on the part of the employee who made the decision, will likely negatively impact the Wine Bus for some time to come. It should have, and could have been avoided if they had used in the abilities in our toolkit.

Related Best Practices of 'Culturally-tuned-in' People:

- ✓ They seek to understand the similarities among cultures, but do not gloss over the differences.
- ✓ They weigh the consequences of their behavior

WORDS TO THRIVE BY

"External actions are evidence of internal thought. Our deeds are what show our creed." Tim Hiller

SHOW ME THE MONEY

Sarah, a 6th grade teacher, is invited to the wedding reception of Radi's father. Radi is a Cambodian student in Sarah's class. When Sarah receives the invitation, she notices there are no notations regarding a registry. Consequently, later that day, Sarah purchases a crystal vase as a gift.

The reception is held at a local Cambodian Restaurant. Someone greets Sarah at the door when she arrives. Sarah hands her the wrapped gift. The woman looks very perplexed, but take the gift and places it on a nearby table. It seems a bit strange to Sarah that there are no other gifts on the table, even though the restaurant appears to be filled almost to capacity.

Sarah is directed to her table, where the first course is about to be served. During the third of six courses, someone comes to each table to collect envelopes from each person. Sarah is very embarrassed when she realizes everyone except herself has an envelope to offer. Sarah later discovers the envelopes contained money, and that it is a Cambodian ritual, and all guests are expected to participate. Sarah is not looking forward to parent conferences, for fear that she will have to relive this faux pas when she apologizes for her ignorance.

How could Sarah have avoided her embarrassment?

TOOLKIT TO THE RESCUE

- **Critical Thinking**

Sarah does not exercise critical thinking. She is attending a familiar type of event, but one of a very different culture. And when she notices the invitation does not include a registry, this should have served as an additional clue that further inquiry was in order.

- **Emotional Intelligence**

As a teacher, Sarah is an educated professional. To earn her degree, basic cultural studies is required. With this knowledge base, Sarah should have been sensitive and caring enough to do her homework, to avoid any major faux pas' that might be viewed as disrespectful.

- **Flexibility**

When attending an event of a culture that is unfamiliar, it is important that those in attendance acquaint themselves with the protocol for that event. There are a number of ways Sarah can accomplish that expectation. She sees Radi five days a week; a simple inquiry would have sufficed.

- **Creativity**

Using online search engines, information about almost any topic is just seconds from reach. Sarah could perform a quick related keyword search, using words such as "multi-cultural weddings" or "Cambodian weddings", to discover more information about Cambodian culture and its traditions.

TEACHABLE MOMENT

In some cultures, traditions require strict compliance as a condition of participation. Failure to comply could be viewed as insulting and or disrespectful. To avoid embarrassment and or denial of participation, take the time to investigate in advance, or decline the invitation.

Related Best Practices of 'Culturally-tuned-in' People

- ✓ They seek to understand the similarities among cultures, but do not gloss over the differences.
- ✓ They value expressions of mutual respect

WORDS TO THRIVE BY

"Failing to plan is planning to fail" Proverb

JUMPING TO CONCLUSIONS

Julio attends a job fair, seeking employment in the tech industry. Since he needs a job right away, Julio decides to also apply outside of his preferred field. He had just completed an application for a small tech firm when he spots the sign, "Hiring Immediately." Although it is a service industry job, he thinks to himself, "What the heck, I need something right away, and I can always keep looking."

Julio approaches the woman at the reception table and requests an application. The woman looks at him, pauses, and replies sharply, "I hope you are legal, because I'm tired of spending my time reviewing applications, only to find out half-way through, that we cannot hire you because you are not legal." Julio's first impulse is to lash out and give the woman a piece of his mind. But he thinks better. Taking a deep breath, Julio smiles and answers, "I am a native born American," and extends his hand for the application.

How could the receptionist benefit from using our toolkit of abilities?

TOOLKIT TO THE RESCUE

- **Critical Thinking**

Testing assumptions is an important component of critical thinking. Had the receptionist been thinking critically, she would not have blurted out the first thing that popped up in her head. Kudos to Julio who was wearing his critical thinking hat and knew that lashing out would be counter-productive.

- **Emotional Intelligence**

Had the receptionist been emotionally-tuned-in, she would have realized that her assumption that Julio was illegal because he appeared to be Mexican could have proven to be wrong, and then become the source of embarrassment for herself and Julio.

Those who invoke their emotional intelligence constantly audit their own emotions, understanding the effects that their emotionally-based reactions have on other people.

- **Flexibility**

Another side benefit of being flexible is the realization that every personal encounter is an opportunity to learn new things about ourselves as well as others. The receptionist's job gives her many opportunities to do just that and in the process, turn potentially negative interactions into positive encounters.

- **Creativity**

Often the most volatile of moments carries the potential to shift energy and change negative to positive results. Exercising a creative option, the receptionist could have re-ordered the questions on the application so that confirming citizenship was addressed first. This approach could also save the time and the frustration of potentially discovering later that the applicant was ineligible to apply for the job.

TEACHABLE MOMENT

Practicing the habit of critical thinking enables practitioners to weigh the consequences of their behavior before they act. In this case the receptionist's outburst could have resulted in a confrontation or a letter to her superiors detailing the negative encounter.

The restraint Julio showed in his reply also shows his emotional intelligence. And the simplicity of a smile is often under-rated, but in terms of honing in on emotional intelligence, it's a 'must-have' in your arsenal.

Related Best Practices of 'Culturally-tuned-in' People

- ✓ They seek to understand the similarities among cultures, but do not gloss over the differences.
- ✓ They value expressions of mutual respect

WORDS TO THRIVE BY

"IQ gets you hired – EQ gets you promoted" – Business newsletter

---

WHAT'S WITH THE COVERUP?

A group of boys at a local swimming pool notice several girls getting out of the pool. This observation in itself is not unusual, except for the fact that the girls are wearing full body swimsuits. As they discuss this observation, one of the boys suggests they must be Muslims. This explanation seems to satisfy all but one of the boys in the group, who replies, "Look at that sign over there. It forbids wearing jeans or cutoffs. So why can they cover up and we can't?" Shrugging the question off, the boys resume their pool activities.

The next day, however, after re-visiting the question regarding cut-offs and jeans at the public pool, the boys returned to the pool donning t-shirts, cut-offs and jeans. When they are denied entrance, the boys protest, noting the presence of girls in full body suits the previous day, and ask, "What's the difference?" The person at the entrance gate states he did not make the rules, and that they should speak to management if they have a problem with the rules.

As luck would have it, the manager is on site. He explains to the boys that the body suits are a form of religious practice, and that religious rights are upheld by the first Amendment of our Constitution. One of the boys then interrupts, saying "We belong to the religious sect of Modesty and Truth, and our laws forbid us from wearing traditional swim attire. So that's why we need to wear non-revealing attire such as you see. The manager laughs, and replies, "Nice try boys, but it ain't happening. I saw you here yesterday wearing Speedos!!"

Which abilities helped the manager finesse the boys' challenge?

TOOLKIT TO THE RESCUE

- **Critical Thinking**

The pool manager, by not allowing the boys to 'push his buttons', showed that that he was already weighing the potential consequences of his optional responses.

- **Emotional Intelligence**

The pool manager drew on his emotional intelligence to understand that using humor, rather than scorn, would probably be the better approach.

- **Flexibility**

By allowing the boys to speak their minds, the pool manager helps maintain an environment that feels inclusive and diverse. It's also a sign that that the manager is comfortable in his leadership role that he can maintain the rules of his establishment while being as flexible as possible.

- **Creativity**

The pool manager seized the opportunity to gives the boys a history lesson.

TEACHABLE MOMENT

First Amendment rights regarding religion have been challenged since their inception. An attempt to establish a clear-cut and absolute definition or ruling has yet to be accomplished, thus the many case laws and citings. While we have focused on the savvy manager, it's worth noting that, in the case of the young teens, a bit of critical thinking could have gone a long way. Googling information on religious rights would have led them to understand that there is a definite difference in the way the Muslim religion, and their self-proclaimed religion would be treated. According to the Newseum Institute[14] at Vanderbilt University's First Amendment Center, there are two basic concepts that generally determine whether or not certain religious rights will be honored:

1. Establish whether or not a person has a claim involving a sincere religious belief
2. Establish whether the government / business actions places a substantial burden on the person's ability to act on that belief.

Without question, the newly created religious sect of Modesty and Truth did not meet the first above stated criteria, thus nullifying the second. The wearing of cut-offs, and jeans was not a sincere religious

[14] Newseuminstitute.org/first-amendment-center/

belief or practice. Taking time to listen to the concern of the boys is not only a good business practice, but it also demonstrates to the boys that they can exercise their first Amendment right to voice their concerns and opinions.

Related Best Practices of 'Culturally-tuned-in' People

- ✓ Seek to understand the similarities among cultures, but do not gloss over the differences.
- ✓ They value expressions of mutual respect
- ✓ They are mindful about how and when they voice their opinions

WORDS TO THRIVE BY

"The purpose of religion is to control yourself, not criticize others" – Dalai Lama

RIGHT VS. RIGHTS

Samuel, a 30ish computer operator, is sitting in the lunchroom with several other co-workers. One of them is Shimir, a female, dressed in the traditional attire for Muslim women. She wears a long sleeve shirt and long skirt, and her hair is covered with a hijab.

Although Samuel and Shimir had previously never really engaged in conversation, they had exchanged pleasantries in passing. As Samuel glances in Shimir's direction, he is reminded of a question that has been on his mind for some time. He decides to direct his question to Shimir: "Shimir, how do you feel about the radical Muslims sect?" Shimir, stunned by the question, hesitates, then replies, "I denounce their behavior, and do not want to be associated with them." This reply leads Samuel to his next question. "If you do not want to be associated with them, then why do you come to work dressed like them?" At this question, Shimir shakes her head and walks away.

Shortly after the encounter, Samuel's supervisor summons him into his office, and closes the door. Samuel is informed that he is out of line. Questioning Shimir about her attire is in essence questioning her religious practice, which is a 1st Amendment Right. After being chastised for his behavior, Samuel is ordered to attend mandatory sensitivity training.

How can our toolkit help Samuel avoid future blunders of this nature?

TOOLKIT TO THE RESCUE

- **Critical Thinking**

Critical thinkers tend to elevate their curiosity with constant study. If Samuel had researched his question prior to asking it, he would have learned that Shimir's attire is a form of religious expression - not a hallmark of radicalism.

- **Emotional Intelligence**

People who develop their emotional intelligence tend to also develop a type of radar that alerts them to the inappropriateness of asking very personal questions – not only with people they barely know but also when they are in the presence of others. In Samuel's situation, he added fuel to the flame by asking Shimir a personally-invasive question in the presence of her co-workers, which is likely why Shimir reported the incident.

- **Flexibility**

Sometimes a situation does not offer many options for a person to demonstrate flexibility. In this instance Samuel has been pondering this question for some time and could have used other avenues, such as contacting a Muslim-base cultural organization, to find answers to his questions. This option would have moved the question from the personal to more generalized tenets – avoiding a situation which in Shimir's instance contributed to her feeling targeted or marginalized.

- **Creativity**

Choosing another path – Asking Shimir the same question in private may not have had much better results. Instead Samuel could have used a creative approach – rephrasing the question so that it didn't feel so hostile or accusatory.

TEACHABLE MOMENT

Even between two people who have a close relationship, the intent of questions that are of an intimate nature can be misconstrued. Consider this advice from two masters of the art of interviewing: Charlie Rose and Barbara Walters. Says Rose, "The question is just as important as the answer". And from Walters: "Don't confuse being stimulating, with being blunt."

Related Best Practices of 'Culturally-tuned-in' People

- ✓ Seek to understand the similarities among cultures, but do not gloss over the differences.
- ✓ They value expressions of mutual respect
- ✓ They are mindful about how and when they voice their opinions

WORDS TO THRIVE BY

"It is not our differences that divide us. It is our inability to recognize, accept and celebrate those differences." Audre Lorde

---

KEEP IT LITE

While sipping wine and sampling hors de oeuvres at a neighborhood gathering, a very diverse group of neighbors enters into a conversation centered around U.S. Immigration policies. Todd, one of the conversationalist, blurts out, "We don't need or want any more immigrants, and I think we should close our borders indefinitely!"

Immediately following Todd's statement, a husband and wife couple politely collect their wraps, leaving the premises with no exchange of words. But if looks could kill, there would have been a massacre!!

Where did Todd fall short of being culturally tuned-in?

TOOLKIT TO THE RESCUE

- **Critical Thinking**

One of the tenets of critical thinking is that no one has a corner on all the right answers – solutions that will keep our planet humming peacefully along. Todd's outburst reveals not only that he hasn't taken the time to sort out all his hidden assumptions and biases. Rather than encourage conversation, his response also is a 'thought stopper' – effectively shutting downs further conversation.

- **Emotional Intelligence**

The jury is still out on whether engaging in conversations involving politics and or religion in mixed company is a worthwhile pursuit. Nevertheless, if Todd was blessed with any degree of emotional intelligence, he would be aware that bringing up these topics, in a way that doesn't offend others in a group setting, takes finesse and considerable forensic skills.

- **Flexibility**

Who hasn't in the heat of discussion found himself starting to say something that is not fully thought-out? If Todd found it difficult to contain his views, he could have exercised some flexibility and excused himself from the group for a brief time until he gave himself a reset.

- **Creativity**

If walking away or excusing himself to re-group was not possible, Todd could have tried dipping into his reservoir of creative abilities and diverting the conversation toward a less controversial topic, like:

"How about those Warriors?" Generally speaking, introducing sports topics are good ways to defuse the 'temperature' of a discussion.

TEACHABLE MOMENT

There is a reason why party hosts known for giving great parties carefully position, by way of table placards, who-sits-next-to-who, at their dinner tables. But even that critically-thought-out strategy loses its initial power once guests mingle at their own discretion. That's the time when the guests with the best set of 'culturally-tuned-in" abilities have the opportunity to shine! And those who don't may suffer some unforgiving social consequences.

Related Best Practices of 'Culturally-tuned-in' People

- ✓ They are mindful about how and when they voice their opinions
- ✓ They value expressions of mutual respect
- ✓ They seek to understand the similarities among cultures, but do not gloss over the differences.

WORDS TO THRIVE BY:

"A conversation, even a brief one, should have all the best features of any functioning human relationships, and that means genuine interest on both sides, opportunity and respect for both to express themselves, and some dashes of tact and perception." – Barbara Walters[15]

GENDER IDENTITY CHALLENGES

THE BLACK LEATHER DRESS

Shannon enters the party rocking a black leather dress, 6 inch heels,

---

[15] Barbara Walters, How to Talk to Practically Anyone About Practically Anything (New York: Doubleday, 1970)

and a neatly groomed beard. Her hair is neatly swept up into a French twist, and ze is ready to party. Another femininely- dressed individual walks up to Shannon and comments, "Girl, you are wearing the hell out of that dress! "Shannon glares at this individual, and replies, "Girl? You called me girl? Honey, you don't know me like that, and you better check yourself!" Then, ze promptly does an about face, and struts away.

At this point, you may be wondering: What just happened?

TOOL KIT TO THE RESCUE

Critical Thinking

The individual who approached Shannon was obviously unaware of Shannon's gender or non-gender preferred identification. A critically thinking person would not have made this gender assumption.

Emotional Intelligence

Emotionally intelligent people are sensitive to situational clues. In this case, the fact that Shannon wore a dress and a beard should have alerted the person to question assumptions regarding Shannon's gender identity.

Flexibility

The person commenting on Shannon's appearance could find an alternate way of complimenting Shannon without attaching a gender label.

Creativity

Simply omitting the word "girl" would have allowed the compliment to stand on its own as gender neutral.

TEACHABLE MOMENT

If you found the reading of this scenario awkward or difficult to follow, then you can understand how the use of gender neutral or non-binary pronouns have resulted in confusion for the population at large. One of the biggest problems facing the adoption of new gender-neutral pronouns is the lack of unity and organization among supporters of this movement that seek to uncouple traditional assumptions about sex and gender identity.

In this scenario, ve, ze, and hir, could have also been acceptable pronouns to use. Shannon, however, like many gender queer people, (this is an acceptable and commonly used title) does not identify with either masculine or feminine genders, but somewhere in-between. Therefore, assigning a gender such as girl, boy, man or woman, could be offensive, and definitely presumptuous. "It is so important to never make assumptions about a person's body or appearance to base a gender pronoun" cautions Steven Petrow[16], journalist who specializes in LGBT etiquette topics.

Laura Kacore, author of *Everyday Feminism*, offers this additional advice: "If a person you are referring to is a stranger or brief acquaintance, you may not need to know their pronoun preference.[17] If the person is a classmate, student, or co-worker, it is best to ask, 'What pronoun do you use?" Or, "How would you like me to refer to you?" Or, "My name is_____ and my pronouns are__ and _____, what about you?"

Related Best Practices of 'Culturally-tuned-in' People

- ✓ They are mindful about how and when they voice their opinions
- ✓ They value expressions of mutual respect
- ✓ They seek to understand the similarities among cultures, but do not gloss over the differences.

WORDS TO THRIVE BY

"Do not judge a book by its' cover" - English idiom

---

[16]Steve Pedrow, GayManners.com
[17] Laura Kacore, Everyday Feminism, (New York: St. Martins Press, 2014)

GET WITH THE PROGRAM

Steven, a local realtor knocks on the door of a prospective listing client. Within moments, a 30ish gentleman invites him in. They sit down at the kitchen table, and begin the question and answer portion of their meeting. As Steven listens to the client, he notices that he often uses the term "we".

Steven precisely remembers the client telling him over the phone that he is the single owner of the property. Being confused, Steven asks," Are there any other individuals on the title to this property?" The client replies, "No." Now Steven is really perplexed, so he replies, "I think you meant to say I, not we." The client promptly with much indignation retorts, "No, I said what I meant."

At this point, Steven begins to visibly show his concern. He isn't sure if he is dealing with a schizophrenic or just someone who wants to play with his head. In any case, the client senses Steven's uneasiness and promptly begins to give him a lesson in the acceptable pronouns to use for what he refers to as genderqueer or non-binary individuals. Steven apologizes for his lack of knowledge regarding the LGBTQ community, and clumsily attempts to salvage the meeting. Noting how uncomfortable and embarrassed Steven appears to be, the client ends the meeting, and shows Steven to the door.

What learnings can our toolkit offer Steven?

TOOL KIT TO THE RESCUE

- **Critical Thinking**

The light bulb does go on when Steven, after a few misfires, understands that there is a communication problem. In this situation, it may be a case of 'too little, too late.'

- **Emotional Intelligence**

Steven did not use his emotional intelligence when inquiring about the client's use of the pronoun, we. Instead of correcting the client's

English, which proved to be somewhat offensive, he could have been more creative in his inquiry.

- **Flexibility**

Steven might not land this client. But this potentially failed encounter may give him cause to think about how he can better structure his conversations in the future.

- **Creativity**

Perhaps Steven could have re-stated the phrase in question, then assign the misunderstanding to himself by asking why he used the term we, if he was the only owner. By doing this, he is not correcting the client, he is simply attempting to make sure he, Steven, has the correct information: His problem, not the client's. This more creative and less offensive response would likely have elicited a less hostile atmosphere, and a much better chance for Steven to land that listing.

TEACHABLE MOMENT

Non-binary pronouns such as we, used in the singular form, in addition to ze, hir, ve, and nem, are singular pronouns that are acceptable in replacing the traditional pronouns of he, she, her, and him, with those identifying with the LGBTQ community. Generally this is because many in the LGBTQ community do not identify with any one gender. In most cases it is accepted and even expected that one inquire as to which term or terms a member of the LGBTQ identifies with.

Related Best Practices of 'Culturally-tuned-in' People

- ✓ They are mindful about how and when they voice their opinions
- ✓ They value expressions of mutual respect
- ✓ They seek to understand the similarities among cultures, but do not gloss over the differences.

WORDS TO THRIVE BY

"Where there's a will, there's a way" American proverb

OPEN MOUTH INSERT FOOT

Jared, a high school principal, agrees to host the end of the school year party at his home. He informs his staff that this year their families are welcome to attend as well.

   At the party, as Jared is mingling with his staff and making introductions, he approaches Bryce, who is standing with his partner Tim, and their two children. He greets them, and proceeds to introduce Bryce, and Tim, 'his husband' to his wife Gwen. Before Jared can go any further, Bryce corrects him, by informing Jared and Gwen that Tim is his wife, not his husband. Jared, very apologetically, accepts the correction, then scurries away in search of the nearest rock!

How differently could Jared have handled this introduction?

TOOL KIT TO THE RESCUE

- **Critical Thinking**

Like sexual orientation, same sex marriages can vary in terms of gender roles. Therefore, because Jared is uncertain in this case, he needs to take a moment and think critically about his options before making this introduction.

- **Emotional Intelligence**

There are indications that Jared is aware that Bryce is gay. If Jared was in-tune to his emotional intelligence, he would not want to say anything that might be embarrassing or offensive.

- **Flexibility**

Bryce's family is not a traditional family. Instead of taking the traditional approach of introduction, Jared needs to step away from his comfort zone, and demonstrate his flexibility. Jared needs an alternate way of addressing Bryce's relationship in his introduction.

- **Creativity**

  Moving into creativity mode, Jared could use a gender free identifier – "significant other", or simply "partner" would fit the criteria.

TEACHABLE MOMENT

Same sex marriages are non-traditional marriages. Therefore, one should not assume that there is either a husband or wife. In some cases, the couples do not subscribe to either term. Instead they identify as partners. In other cases, there could be two moms or two dads in the relationship. Unless there is certainty of the preferred identification, avoid making assumptions and references to gender.

Related Best Practices of 'Culturally-tuned-in' People

- ✓ They seek to understand the similarities among cultures, but they do not gloss over the differences.
- ✓ They value expressions of mutual respect.

WORDS TO THRIVE BY

"Loose lips sink ships." English Proverb

THE DOOR SWINGS BOTH WAYS

Madison attends a business luncheon at a local restaurant with four male co-workers. As they approach the door of the restaurant, Madison finds herself in front of the group and the first one to reach the door. Madison pauses for a moment. She is not sure if she should open the door for herself, or wait for her male co-worker behind her to do the honors. Where are the automated doors when you need them?

How can Madison use the abilities in our toolkit to her advantage?

TOOL KIT TO THE RESCUE

- **Critical Thinking**

When Madison paused at the door, she was in essence reaching into her tool-kit for the element of critical thinking. Madison is aware that she must make a quick decision. Should she open the door for herself or wait for her male co-worker?

- **Emotional Intelligence**

Madison may or may not be aware of the suggested response, according to noted experts in etiquette[18]. However Madison's emotional quotient once activated will alert her that most people are rarely offended by a kind gesture.

- **Flexibility**

Often when a woman approaches a door before a man, he will allow her to open the door part of the way, then take over, and complete the act. Therefore, Madison just needs to be flexible and go with the flow. If one of the men does not step in front to open the door, then Madison should open it.

- **Creativity**

Accessing her creativity skill, Madison could simply turn her dilemma into an act of kindness, by opening the door and holding it open for all in her party.

TEACHABLE MOMENT

---

[18] EmilyPost.com/Revolving door: Who Goes First?

In the article, "The Ins and Outs of Opening a Door for a Woman."[19] Brett and Kate McKay state, "It doesn't matter whether you are a man or woman, offering to hold the door open for the other person, is respectful and friendly."

Related Best Practices of 'Culturally-tuned-in' People

✓ They value expressions of mutual respect.

✓ They weigh the consequences of their behavior

WORDS TO THRIVE BY

"Everyone in the world is somehow connected. So why not just be nice to everyone?" Richard Simmons

SHIFTING PERSONAL BOUNDARIES IN PUBLIC SPACES

TO PEE OR NOT TO PEE

Jake enters the men's room, approaches the urinal, begins to unzip his pants, but hesitates when he notices the man standing to his right, is peering at him. Jake glances at him and the man smiles sheepishly. Jake's comfort level drops from 10 to zero instantly. He had not started his business, and at this point, he is not sure if he should.

At this point what are Jake's options?

TOOL KIT TO THE RESCUE

- **Critical Thinking**

Jake has begun to think critically, because he is questioning his next move.

- **Emotional Intelligence**

[19] Brett and Kay McKay, Artofmanliness.com/category/a-mans-life/

A glance and a smile might be inadvertent. It is likely that Jake took this into consideration when he chose to avoid any form of verbal exchange.

- **Flexibility**

Jake realizes he has at least two viable choices: He can be flexible and forego the use of the urinal, or ignore the alleged on-looker, and complete his business.

- **Creativity**

Jake quickly looks around and sees a vacant stall. He enters the stall where he can complete his business in privacy. Mission accomplished!

TEACHABLE MOMENT

There is no question that times have changed regarding what is, and is not acceptable among the sexes. With the increase and acceptance of gender re-assignment, transgender and gender-neutral identifications, gender-free public facilities, as a result, may present some unexpected challenges that must be navigated with thought and care. Using your 'culturally-tuned-in' toolkit will help guide you through this journey.

Related Best Practices of 'Culturally-tuned-in' People

✓ They are sensitive to the boundaries of personal space, their own and others.
✓ They weigh the consequences of their behavior.

WORDS TO THRIVE BY

"The Best defense is a good offense." - Jack Dempsey

YOU ARE NOT A HOLOGRAM

Mitchell and Allesse are the proud parents of a daughter who dances competitively at many competitions and recitals. These events are generally very enjoyable, with one exception - The parents and relatives who block the view of others while taking photos and videoing their child/children's performance. Mitchell and Allesse have shared their concerns between themselves, but have not taken their concerns any further.

Which abilities from our tool kit can help Mitchell and Allesse resolve their issue?

TOOL KIT TO THE RESCUE

- **Critical Thinking**

Mitchell and Allesse, using the critical thinking process, have identified the problem and are seeking a resolution for themselves and others, who likely have similar concerns.

- **Emotional Intelligence**

In this instance, it is very likely that it is Mitchell and Allesse's emotional intelligence that has allowed them to suffer in silence, each time they encounter this issue. They empathize with the offensive parents, relatives, and friends, because they understand the desire to capture and savor those precious proud moments.

- **Flexibility**

Due to the scope of the problem, it is not feasible for Mitchell and Allesse to handle it on their own. Confronting the offending picture takers would likely yield little or no results, and might actually make matters worse. Rather than attempting to solve the dilemma on their own, they might engage the help of the studio owners who can communicate the concern universally with parents, thus avoiding singling out any one offender.

- **Creativity**

Additionally Mitchell and Allesse could provide some suggestions to their studio director – Such as hiring a photographer/videographer to exclusively capture the event or as a less restrictive solution – providing a designated section for photography and videoing that does not impede the audience's sightlines.

TEACHABLE MOMENT

Whenever possible, engage the help of those with the power to effect change.

Related Best Practices of 'Culturally-tuned-in' People:

✓ They are sensitive to the boundaries of personal space; their own and others
✓ They value the expression of mutual respect

WORDS TO THRIVE BY

"Manners maketh the man"   Proverbs

TOO CLOSE FOR COMFORT

Owen walks up to the ATM machine outside of his community bank. He wants to withdraw cash from his account. Prior to beginning his transaction, he senses the person behind him move forward. Owen feels his privacy is being compromised. He does not feel comfortable completing the transaction. There is a line of people waiting, and he really needs the cash.

How can Owen take advantage of our toolkit?

TOOLKIT TO THE RESCUE

- **Critical thinking**

Owen quickly utilizes his habit of critical thinking. He realizes that continuing his transaction could result in a breach of his privacy, which ultimately could allow someone to gain access to his account.

- **Emotional Intelligence**

It's possible that the person in back of Owen could have inadvertently moved forward, having no intentions of breaching Owen's privacy. It is also possible that it was intentional with sinister motives. In either case, Owen's emotional intelligence should prompt him to take caution, and avoid addressing the person –possibly provoking a confrontational response

- **.Flexibility**

Owen should be flexible. He cannot take the chance of having his privacy compromised. If possible Owen should access another ATM machine at a different location.

- **Creativity**

If time is not a factor, Owen could act creatively. He could offer the person directly behind him to access the ATM machine first. If that person has malicious motives, they have been foiled. If the person had no bad intentions, then Owen has at least eliminated the source of his concern.

TEACHABLE MOMENT

Automation, like it or not, is here to stay. Banks, grocery stores, gas station etc. have all taken advantage of the latest technology. The rules governing our behavior in these public places, as we take advantage of these conveniences, are ever changing. The ATM machine in particular, offers a unique challenge - Specifically, the proper etiquette regarding standing distance. Generally speaking, a distance of 8-10 feet is currently acceptable.

Related Best Practices of 'Culturally-tuned-in' People:

- ✓ They are sensitive to the boundaries of personal space; their own and others.
- ✓ They weigh the consequences of their behavior.

WORDS TO THRIVE BY

"An ounce of prevention is worth a pound of cure." Benjamin Franklin

---

MANSPREAD: TWO FOR THE PRICE OF ONE

Shana boards a train in her local rapid transit system. All of the seats appear to be taken, so she and another passenger stand, holding on to a vertical pole to steady themselves. As Shana scans her surroundings, she notices three seats that are made to seat two passengers. Each is occupied by one man, whose legs are spread so far apart, that they do not allow room for a second passenger to be seated. Shana is tired and has several packages. She would really like to sit down, but her dilemma is how to accomplish that goal.

How can our toolkit help Shana in this situation?

TOOLKIT TO THE RESCUE

- **Critical Thinking**

Critical thinking helps Shana acknowledge her dilemma, and assess her options.

- **Emotional Intelligence**

Often emotional intelligence boils down to gauging non-verbal cues. Shana could try to catch the eye of each of the men in question, smile, and observe their body language to determine the best candidate to approach.

- **Flexibility**

If one of the men in question moves over, Shana should consider his reply to her question, and his body language to determine whether or not she should sit down in the seat with her bags, or just set her bags on the seat. In either case, Shana's situation will improve. Being accepting of either outcome demonstrates flexibility.

- **Creativity**

If one or more of the men return her smile, that is an indicator of approachability. She might ask, "Would you mind if I share some of your space?"

TEACHABLE MOMENT

Manspread, and the general sprawling of belongings such as backpacks, purses, and briefcases onto un-occupied seating is a common issue. It's one of the subjects tackled in New York City's *Courtesy Counts* campaign – a series of instructive posters mounted in its subways. Who hasn't had the experience of attending an event with limited available seating, where many of the seats are occupied not by patrons, but rather the belonging of patrons? How to handle the situation will vary depending on the setting. Being able to draw from our toolkit gives practitioners a definite advantage in many very diverse situations.

Related Best Practices of 'Culturally-tuned-in' People:

- ✓ They are sensitive to the boundaries of personal space; their own and others.

- ✓ They weigh the consequences of their behavior

WORDS TO THRIVE BY

" Be sincere, Be brief, Be seated."   Franklin Roosevelt

BUMP THAT STICKER

Dr. Phelps, the Superintendent of the Sun Valley School District, is making one of his monthly school site visits. He parks his car in the parking lot designated for teachers only. As he walks through the parking lot, he notices a car with a bumper sticker that reads, " Zero to Bitch in 10 seconds." As he proceeds through the parking lot, he witnesses several sexually suggestive bumper stickers. When he enters the office of the principal, he mentally adds another item to his agenda that must be addressed!

What does that bumper sticker also say about its owner?

TOOL KIT TO THE RESCUE

- **Critical Thinking**

There's a definite disconnect between the way that the bumper sticker's owner perceives herself outside of her work environment and her role in her professional capacity. Prior to applying the bumper sticker to her car, applying a bit of critical thinking would have gone a long way for this teacher as well as the other teachers with suggestive bumper stickers. The rule that applies to students - that certain language, phrases and terms are forbidden on campus--- also apply to them.

- **Emotional Intelligence**

Teachers are expected to be models of acceptable behavior on campus. Failing to do live up to that standard sends mixed messages to students and creates a domino effect. This ultimately challenges the validity of the rules. Challenging rules promotes discord, thus upsetting the educational process. Educating is the primary responsibility of teachers. Anything that impedes the task, brings into question the integrity of the teacher.

- **Flexibility**

When off campus, the bumper stickers might be perfectly acceptable. The challenge here is to find a way to keep the bumper sticker, but refrain from displaying it while on campus.

- **Creativity**

One creative option could be to use a car cover while on campus. If a cover is not an option, parking a short distance from campus would suffice.

TEACHABLE MOMENT

Freedom of speech, in both written and verbal form, are basic rights spelled out in our Constitution's Bill of Rights. However, there are no assurances that there will not be consequences attached

Related Best Practices of 'Culturally-tuned-in' People:

- ✓ They weigh the consequences of their behavior
- ✓ They are mindful about how they voice their opinions

WORDS TO THRIVE BY

"If you cannot be good, be careful"   Proverb

Conclusion

We hope you have found *The Don't Get Me Started! Toolkit* to be informative, thought-provoking and even entertaining! When we first started writing this book, we knew that just being able to capture the scope of the challenges facing folks today would in itself be a big challenge. And that it wouldn't be easy to capture the complex nature of situations that folks encounter today.

But in our quest to vividly describe these challenges, there may be some readers who wonder if our renderings are too negative: Hasn't technology really improved our lives? Don't all generations tend to misunderstand each other? In advocating for considered and often considerate responses to situations, doesn't our toolkit encourage even greater political correctness at the expense of our true feelings?

Yes! With an asterisk

We would say "Yes" -----but go a few steps further. For all its weak links, there is no doubt that social media has empowered people in unprecedented ways – enabling them to communicate with each other across the once traditional barriers mounted by entrenched powers-that-be. And thanks to the convergence of broadband networks and 'Big Data', transgender folks who want to use the rest room that is in sync with their gender identity can locate 'gender-free' restrooms, courtesy of such resources like the online Refuge Restroom database.

We argue that there may be no other time in history when so many people from so many different economic, political and social strata have the technological tools at their fingertips to affect change in their lives. What we address in *The Don't Get Me Started! Toolkit* is the gap between the potential of these tools and the behaviors needed to achieve results in a win-win way.

And to those who argue that 'political correctness' has gone "too far" we offer this response: If you believe in the principle that barriers to racial, social class, and gender equality should not exist in a socially-just world –you will not only be politically correct but culturally tuned-in.

The will to change when no one is keeping score

Naysaying observers of the human condition may speculate whether the will to change has gone the way of rotary telephones and other relics of a bygone era. We think that the will and desire to excel is definitely evident in the chase for excellence in sports and commerce. But when it comes to day to day living, when what's at stake is taking place outside the ball court or the boardroom – when no one is keeping score - we see less emphasis on the importance of striving for more critical thinking, emotional intelligence and the willingness to go outside the comfort zone and try creative and flexible approaches to problem solving.

   If it does nothing else, we hope that *The Don't Get Me Started! Toolkit* will spark more conversations about changing that tide – motivating our readers to give our toolkit a chance in their daily lives. Let us know if it makes a difference in your life.

Connect with us:

Twitter: @DGetMeStarted

Facebook: The Don't Get Me Started Toolkit

Email: dgmskp@gmail.com

Resources

We live in an age where people on earth have unparalleled access to information, largely thanks to the ubiquitous use of the Internet. By no means an exhaustive list, in this section we identify just a few resources that can help our readers dive deeper into the major concepts we discuss in *The Don't Get Me Started! Toolkit* .

Cultural Challenges

- Rapid Advances in Technology

Just about every aspect of our lives has been impacted by technological changes. These advances have far outstripped many users' abilities to comprehend the impact –both beneficial and destructive – that these new connection 'opportunities' represent in their lives.

The following resources do an excellent job of not only interpreting these changes but predicting their impacts in the years to come.

Books:

Gilder, George. *Microcosm: The Quantum Revolution in Economics and Technology.* A Touchstone Book, 1990

Gilder, George. *Telecosm: The World After Bandwidth Abundance.* FreePress, 2002.

Kelly, Kevin. *The Inevitable – Understanding the 12 Technological Forces That Will Shape Our Future.* New York: Viking, 2016.

Kurzweil, Ray. *The Age of Spiritual Machines: When Computers Exceed*

Human Intelligence. New York: Penguin Books, 1999

Ronson, Jon. *So You've been Publicly Shamed.* Riverhead Books, 2015.

Websites:

Mashable.com

TechCrunch.com

Pew Research.org

Venturebeat.com

Podcasts/Videos

Abha Dawesar: Life in the Digital Now (Video- Ted Talk)

Curiositystream.com (podcasts)

• Generational and Ethnic Differences

The generational "fault lines" are shifting. Forces contributing to this shifting are rooted in three main factors: Computerization that has transformed both work and play environments; Dramatic economic cycles of boom and bust that upset traditional predictions and changing value systems that challenge traditional mores.

Books:

Graham Brown. *The Mobile Youth: Voices of The Mobile Generation.* mobileYouth, 2014.

Kriegel, Jessica. *Unfairly Labeled – How Your Workplace Can Benefit from*

Ditching Generational Stereotypes. Wiley, 2016

McBride, Tom and Nief, Ron. *The Mindset List of the Obscure.* Sourcebooks, 2014

Tabscott, Don. *Grown Up Digital: How the Net Generation Is Changing Your World* . McGraw-Hill Education, 2008.

Websites:

Diversityandinclusionatwork.com

The Mindset List (www.beloit.edu/mindlist)

Podcasts/Videos

Freakonomics Radio

De-Coding the next generation | Michael McQueen | TEDxNorthernSydneyInstitute

   People are far more likely to live in communities that are more culturally diverse than when and where they were born or grew up. According to a Pew Research Center report, immigration is projected to be the key driver of national population growth in the coming half century, based on the expectation that immigrants tend to have higher birth rates than native born residents. Assimilating these new residents with established citizens presents challenges in the workplace and public spaces, especially when immigrants' cultural traditions clash with those of their new communities.

Books:

Fadiman, Ann. *The Spirit Catches You and You Fall Down: A Hmong Child, Her American Doctors, and the Collision of Two Cultures,* Farrar, Straus and Giroux, 2012

Jane Hyun. *Flex: The New Playbook for Managing Across Differences.* HarperBusiness, 2014

Morrison, Terri. *Kiss, Bow or Shake Hands.* Adams Media, 2006

.

Websites:

Global Issues.org

Migrationpolicy.org

Institute for Social Policy and Understanding

Podcasts/Videos

Understanding Immigration Issues

Harvard Humanitarian Initiative: Refugee Crisis Podcasts

Moral Courage Channel

- Evolving Gender Identity Challenges

The binary model that has defined the traditional constructs of male vs.female is being challenged by the transgender movement. As the boundaries of these definitions blur, society is struggling with the ramifications that come into play in both the public and private spheres.

Books:

Ehrensaft PhD, Diane and Menvielle MD MSHS, Edgardo. *Gender Born, Gender Made: Raising Healthy Gender-Nonconforming Children.* The Experiment, 2011

Howell, Ally Windsor. *Transgender Persons and the Law.* American Bar Association, 2016

Websites:

Gay Manners.com

Gender and Gender Identity (Planned Parenthood.org)

Answers to Your Questions About Transgender People, Gender Identity and Gender Expression (American Psychological Association)

Podcasts/Videos

The Gay Agenda Show

Equally Speaking

Trans-Ponder

- Shifting Personal Boundaries in Public Spaces

In what are commonly considered 'public' spaces, people are increasingly behaving in ways that in previous times would be relegated to 'private' spaces. This is a phenomenon partly due to changes in social communication patterns as well as wide-spread adoption of new technologies. Judging from the often 'cluelessness' of their behavior in both physical and virtual public spaces, it is apparent to us that people are only in the *very* nascent stages of sorting out how to respect the invisible yet very real private boundaries that surround people when they are inhabiting public spaces.

Books:

Agger, Ben. *Oversharing: Presentations of Self in the Internet Age (Framing 21st Century Social Issues)* Routledge, 2015.

Ellard, Colin. *Places of the Heart: The Psychogeography of Everyday Life.* Bellevue Literary Press, 2015

Spehr, Karen and Curnow, Rob. *Litter-ology: Understanding Littering and the Secrets to Clean Public Places* . Environment Books, 2015

Websites:

Pew Research.org: Privacy in 2025-Experts' Predictions

Behavior in Public Places: Teach Your Child Good Behavior (Summit Medical Group)

Podcasts/Videos:

Cellphone Classroom Etiquette (YouTube)

- *The Don't Get Me Started! Toolkit* and Best Practices

Books:

Baker, Aspen. *Pro-Voice, How to Keep Listening When The World Wants to Fight.* Berrett-Koehler Publishers, 2015

Cain, Susan. *Quiet: The Power of Introverts in a World That Can't Stop Talking.* Broadway Books, 2013.

Kleinman, Arthur. *What Really Matters.* Oxford University Press, 2007

Paul, Richard and Elder Linda. *Critical Thinking: Tools for Taking Charge of Your Learning and Your Life.* FT Press, 2002

Rigie, Mitchell and Harmeyer, Keith. *Smartstorming.* Dog Ear Publishing, 2013

Segler, Harvey. *Critical Thinking: Powerful Strategies That Will Make You Improve Decisions And Think Smarter.* Amazon Digital Services, 2015

Sobel. Andrew and Panas, Jerold. *Power Questions: Build Relationships, Win New Business, and Influence Others.* Wiley, 2012.

Tuhovsky, Ian. *Emotional Intelligence: A Practical Guide to Making Friends with Your Emotions and Raising Your EQ.* Amazon Digital Services, 2015

Websites:

Characteristics of Highly Creative People (The Creativity Post)

The Critical Thinking Community

Critical Thinking on the Web

Test Your Emotional Intelligence

Podcasts/Videos:

Critical Thinking Crash Course by Dr. Peter Boghossian

Daniel Dennett on Tools To Transform Our Thinking

Emotional Intelligence - Why Your EQ Is More Important Than Your IQ

About the Authors

Connie Payne and Patricia Kutza bring to the making of *The Don't Get Me Started! Toolkit: Strategies for a Culturally-Challenged World* over thirty years of experience each in the education (Payne) and telecom (Kutza) sectors. This book draws on their personal experiences as well as primary and secondary research in the following disciplines: psychology, ethics, law, sociology and technology.

Connect with us:

Twitter: @DGetMeStarted

Facebook: The Don't Get Me Started Toolkit

Email: dgmskp@gmail.com

www.ingramcontent.com/pod-product-compliance
Lightning Source LLC
Chambersburg PA
CBHW060910280326
41934CB00007B/1264